BREWERY OPERATIONS MANUAL

---

3 STEPS

TO OPEN AND RUN A SUCCESSFUL BREWERY

TOM HENNESSY

Brewery and Operations Manual.
3 Steps to Open and Run a Successful Brewery

ISBN 978-0-9861362-0-7

www.breweryoperationsmanual.com

For Sandy

Contents

STEP 3

THE BUSINESS SYSTEM

Introduction

One hundred years ago there were about 2,000 breweries in the United States. In 2011 we past that number but just think of what the population is in the U.S. compared to then! There is a lot of room for growth.

I own a successful little brewpub in a town of about 800 people in it. I often think of how many towns there are across the globe with a population of at least that much. Heck, there are plenty of buildings in big cities with a population greater than our little town! I think every town deserves to have its own brewery, just like having its own coffee house, or bakery, or clothing store.

We still have a long way to go to even reach an equal amount of wineries (about 7,000). My point is that there is a long way to go before we have saturated the market. So there is no reason you also cannot put a brewery in your town. It is my hope that this little manual becomes a valuable tool you for you to use to add your brewery to that current total.

At this point, I have opened six breweries of my own, and helped with over 50 others. Because I am essentially cheap, I did them for just a fraction of what the "professionals" say you need. Our breweries have made what I think is really good beer, winning medals and awards at the Great American Beer Festival and World Beer Cup.

Here is what I have found along the way. Once you understand the basics, starting and running a moneymaking brewery is really not so difficult. To that end, I have developed a simple set of steps that you can follow to take you beyond the dreaming stage and into your own brewery in about six months.

This manual is designed to be a practical guide through all the steps necessary to open your own brewery. Keep in mind that your location will dictate specific requirements. A small town in Ohio will be different from the big island of Hawaii. States and counties have their own rules and you will have to follow them. It is up to you to find these out. I can guide you through the rest.

What I am giving you is your to-do list. Some sections can be rather short and simple while others lengthy and in depth. The starting point will be money, of course. Once you have a handle on that, you can move forward and put your plan together. It may be that your biggest question is the type of equipment to buy and how to put the equipment together. However, this manual will cover so much more! Including: the type of location for your business, the setup of your business and finally the systems to run a lucrative operation.

STEP 1

THE SET UP

Chapter 1

MONEY

This is really your starting point. Without cash resources all you can do is dream and plan. It is time to gather your resources and investment capital. That means your own, and any other cash you can scrounge up.

In this chapter we'll go through all the obvious sources of capital and some that maybe you haven't thought of. The first giant step will get you over this initial stumbling block so that everything else can happen, so hang in there. It shouldn't be too painful.

The Big Nut

Our goal is to build this brewery for anywhere between $50,000 and $100,000. It could cost you a lot more depending on location and how complicated a brewery you open but for now I want to start with a simple set up. You can or subtract to this as you see fit. So let's get started building our budget.

Your Funds

Junk

You may have more than you know. Start by listing any personal assets that can be turned into cash. Even garage sale items can net you a cool thousand. In fact you can organize a neighborhood sale that you manage and keep 10% of the stuff you sell that is not yours. This money can be used as your seed money to purchase your own stock in your company. Because no matter how small you start, the IRS wants to see some of your money invested in your company. That could be as little as one or two thousand dollars. The rest can be borrowed.

Savings

This may not even be in a traditional savings account. It could be a little extra cash in your checking. Or it could be some old savings bonds that your great aunt left you. Think about your 401k and any IRA's you have. Are you willing to take the tax hit and cash these in? You may have stock funds that are performing poorly, and could be better invested in your own stock. At least you will have control over it compared to the companies you are currently invested in.

Assets

These are your larger items such as jet skis, an extra car, a vintage guitar, or motorcycle. And yes, even your house. Some are items you could just sell outright because you don't need them. Be willing to let go of some of these things to realize the primary goal and find the cash to see your own brewery desires fulfilled.

It may be possible to pull some equity out of your own home, or you may decide to sell the house outright and rent for a while. Based on how much you can pull from the sale of your junk, your savings and assets, it may give you more comfort to leave your house out of the equation.

So hopefully at this point, you have around $10,000 to $20,000. If you used your house and 401K maybe even $50,000 or $75,000.

Getting rid of things you didn't really need may leave you feeling quite liberated. Now you basically have enough to purchase real brewing equipment and that can be used as leverage to get more cash later on.

Trades

To build your brewery will involve lawyers, accountants, plumbers, electricians, welders, and contractors. Compared to building a dentist office, this could be fun for them. You may even already know some of these people and can work special deals with them.

For example, your lawyer and accountant buddies may just do the work in trade for beer. Yes, beer sometimes is more valuable than money. Breweries are such cool projects and they become a nice break for these folks. They will want to be involved.

Basic labor such as the demolition on your space or other general labor can be done by a group of friends. Just make sure you keep a keg on tap at the work site (but not tapped until the work is finished).

The plumbing, electrical, and general contractors should also be approached to see if they could discount their bill in part for trade. For example they may be having Christmas parties or summer picnics and will need kegs or a place to have their party. They could also just discount a certain amount and they can then run a tab when they come in.

You will still have to pay any taxes incurred by these trades. Your accountant can tell you how to track these.

Your total from all the trades could easily equal five to ten thousand dollars. Assuming you managed to scrounge up $20,000 your total now with your own money is close to $30,000.

Family and Friends

You knew sooner or later you might be hitting them up! If you are lucky, some of your friends or relatives may have already approached you with an offer of financial help. The others are just not answering their phones and hoping you won't call. When and if the time comes, it is important to realize you are not coming to them empty-handed. This will be a real business with cash flow and you can afford to give them a return on their investment.

The bad economy works in your favor. Interest rates are so low that any investments your family or friends have may only pay one or two percent. The deal you work out for them will be much sweeter.

Take blocks of no less than $5,000. You may need only three investors at $25,000 or 15 investors at $5,000, but don't go for amounts that are any less or there will be too many people involved. Have a lawyer write up a loan agreement that is flexible with its payments. You may want to consider interest only for the first six months at 5%, and eventually go to 10% interest only, and finally move up to 10% principal and interest accrued on a monthly basis. This will keep your payments low at the beginning as you build your business. The investors are getting a monthly check that is way higher than any other investments they could make.

If you need to sweeten the pot in addition to their monthly check, they may also be entitled to a share of the profits. This is called phantom stock. They do not actually own stock, but they are entitled to a share of declared profits as though they actually owned stock. This continues until the loan is paid off.

But wait there's more! You can also give them a monthly tab, so they can drink beer for free. Keep it small, about $100 or so per month. This keeps them coming in and gives them a sense of being invested and they can keep an eye on their investment.

Depending on the total cost of the brewery, you can also offer your equipment as security against these loans. Used brewing equipment does not depreciate. If you spend $30,000 on your equipment, that can be liquidated if the whole thing falls apart and your investors will be the first in line to be paid. That means that their exposure is limited.

This is a really good deal for your investors and the best part is you don't have to go to a bank for your business loan. That does not mean that this loan isn't just as serious of course. In fact it is more personal as you are getting money from your loved ones instead of an impersonal bank. And because you are personally involved with your investors, you have a deep incentive to make your brewery a success.

The Bank

Last but not least is your bank. If you have plenty of equity in your home, a small bank loan should not be too big an issue. If on the other hand you are renting an apartment, and have no collateral, you will most likely need to get a Small Business Administration (SBA) loan.

In a SBA loan, the bank is still loaning the money to you, but the SBA is guaranteeing the loan. In effect, it is providing the collateral for the bank. But, as it is the government, there is a lot of paperwork involved, and they will run you through the hoops.

Their web site, www.sba.gov, is actually very good and has plenty of tools for writing a business plan, and all the financial templates you will need to fill out their applications. There is much to learn from their web site and much of it very helpful. The main thing you may learn is that you would rather use your friends and family.

Your Landlord

Assuming that you are going to rent your location, you can save part of your opening budget by negotiating rent or tenant improvements with your new landlord.

At a minimum I like to ask for free rent during construction and opening. This could last up to 6 months. If your landlord balks at this you can negotiate it down to half rent, which is very reasonable and could save you a bunch.

Another possibility is to ask for a tenant improvement allowance. This could be one or two dollars per square foot to help defray the cost of improving their building. With new lease spaces, this is pretty common. However, if you are just renting an existing restaurant (which I recommend), the landlord may not have the ability to give you a check.

You might consider asking for a tenant improvement allowance to be amortized over the course of your lease in rent reduction. You still get the cash benefit, but it is spread out over the length of your lease, so it doesn't hurt the landlord too much, and is very reasonable.

The combination of any of these factors could save you around $5,000 off the cost of your opening expenses. It is well worth the effort.

The Final Result

Assuming this is going to be a $100,000 brewery, this would be the breakdown.

Your Personal Cash $15,000
Family & Friends Loans $75,000
Trades $ 5,000
Landlord Breaks $ 5,000
Total $100,000

Of course this is just one of any number of scenarios. Possibly your project may cost less, depending on the type and condition of the space you are renting. I did an Italian restaurant in Santa Fe, N.M. that only cost me $80,000 to open. The previous tenants spent $800,000, and it was so nice that I only had to do basic renovations. Although I sold the restaurant eventually, it did over $2,000,000 per year and Pranzo Italian Grill is still in business over twenty five years later.

You may also choose to do a bare-bones brewery serving only beer in a very simple space at a cost of $50,000. We'll get into these different scenarios later, but you can see that only needing $50,000 changes the odds on coming up with the funds.

So just to go over it again; step one in this process is to gather your funds. Once you feel comfortable in knowing that you will be able to pay for your brewery, you can now go on to find your location. Other than money, it is the location that drives the whole process. The right location will dictate what type of brewery you do. In the next chapter I'll go over the specifics of what to look for that will save you the most money, and help assure your success.

Chapter 2

LOCATION

A giant step forward is first to not need as much money for your project; hence the purpose of this book and the essence of this next chapter.

Having enough money, or being in possession of brewing equipment, pale in comparison to finding the right location for your brewery.

First find an existing restaurant for rent or to purchase. Given the turnover rate in the restaurant business this is easier than you think.

There is nothing cut and dried about this however. It is very personal and reflects your ideas about what you want to do. In this chapter I'll go over all the specifics of what to look for and what will save you the most money and time in your brewery build-out. The actual location is up to you, and your knowledge of your town

There are formulas and certain "do's and don'ts" that the pros follow, but nothing can replace local knowledge. In fact I have a confession to make right up front; I never do much in the way of analysis when scouting a location. Oh sure I check on crime rates, education and income levels. Checking traffic is good too, but it is my gut that tells me "yes, this is the place". I'm not expecting you to follow this intuitive approach, but rather take it as another piece of information. Hopefully this and your own gut instincts will guide you to the perfect location for you.

Get Thee To A Restaurant

The first, best thing is to find an existing restaurant that is for lease or for sale. Even when the economy is good, the turnover rate in restaurants is almost off the charts (don't worry, you are opening a brewpub or brewery, which is a different animal). Having said that, there are always restaurants available.

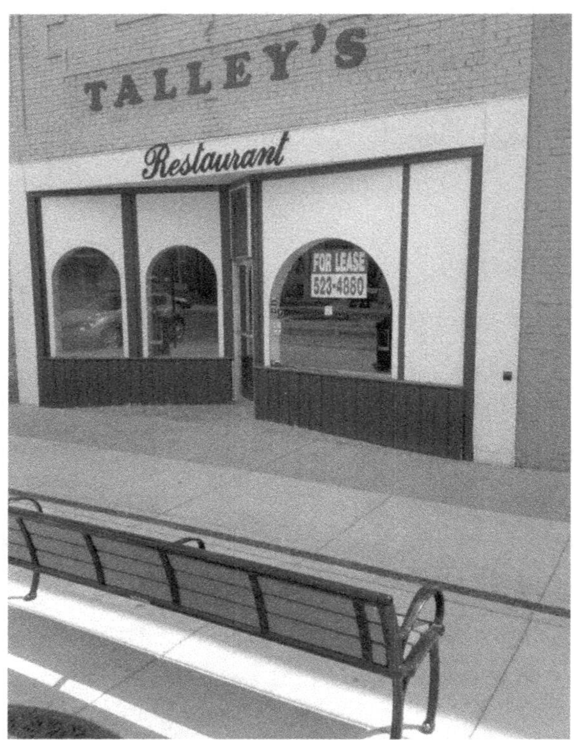

Perfect Location in a Busy Downtown

There are obvious advantages to using an existing restaurant for your brewery. You will find:

- Floor drains and floor sinks in place
- Restrooms that are likely handicap accessible
- Walk-in coolers
- Commercial kitchen space
- Air-conditioning and heating systems
- Commercial hot water heaters
- Grease traps plumbed in
- Adequate electrical amperage for your needs
- Parking

Best of all, these restaurants are likely zoned commercial and have been brought up to code at some point in the recent past.

By having **floor drains** and sinks already in place, it may be possible to use them in the location they are in and avoid having to cut through the floor and install new ones. In fact, if you use the kitchen for your brew-house, the flooring should be perfect. You can even place the kettle under the existing hood, which could save you quite a bit on the type of kettle you choose and how it is hooked up. Plus the kitchen area usually has the type of floor that you can get wet, which happens a lot in a brewery.

Restrooms cost a lot of money to install if there are none or only one in the building you may be interested in. With a restaurant, there are already two, plus maybe even a third for the staff's use. If the restaurant that you find is not too old, the restrooms should be up to code, meaning that they are the right size to be handicap accessible, with grab-bars and proper sinks. If this is the case, then you can just remodel the rooms to make it more befitting a brewery or your own decorating tastes.

If you are lucky, there may be a **walk-in cooler** in the restaurant you have found. You may be able to store your conditioning tanks in it. If it is not big enough, then you can still store kegs, hops, and any food items you may be selling in your light menu.

Not only is an existing **kitchen space** good if you locate the brew-house in it, but the plumbing is already there for some of the other things you will need, such as a mop sink, dish washing area, chemical storage, dry-goods storage, and usually an office off to the side.

Speaking of which, an office in a restaurant is usually already wired for phones, satellite TV, and music systems. There may even already be a floor safe in there.

If you rent just a regular commercial space, it may have just enough **heating and cooling** to handle the bare minimum for the amount of square footage. In a restaurant these are maximized to handle large crowds of customers. This works well for you as you may also have large crowds, but in addition enough air moving to satisfy the 200,000 BTU gas-fired burner you will need to heat your brew kettle. That saves on having an engineer working a very expensive new HVAC (heating, ventilation, air conditioning) system into your brewery.

If you plan to serve some food in your brewery, the local health department will have you calculate your hot water needs. This usually dictates a **commercial hot water heater**, as compared to a domestic one. These are expensive units so why put out that kind of money if you don't have to?

And speaking of the health department, another thing you will need in order to serve food is a **grease trap**. This is a box that is mounted in-line in your drains going from your dish area to where the drain line exits the building. As grease is heavier than water, it is "trapped" in this box so that it doesn't continue into the sewer system, eventually clogging all the pipes in your neighborhood. Your health department will tell you how big your trap has to be, but if there is already one there…

Breweries use a lot of power, and so do restaurants. You could get away with a 200-amp service to your brewery, but 400 would allow you more flexibility. Many restaurants are usually wired for **greater electrical capacity** because of the large refrigeration loads. Upgrading your power is an expense that would be smart to avoid.

The space may also be wired for three-phase electric as compared to a typical single-phase electric supply. This would be a big plus as it costs less to run. If you have three-phase, it would also mean that your electric motors on your equipment would also have to be three-phase. You are not likely to find this in a restaurant however, and in the long run it is not that big of a deal but something that you should be aware of.

At Colorado Boy Brewery we only have a 200-amp service that is single phase. So far it has met the needs of our small establishment. Any regular size restaurant you find will most likely have 400-amp service unless the restaurant has not been renovated since 1921.

The previous tenants of a restaurant space were probably required by the city to provide **adequate parking** for their business. This means paved with curbs and lighting. Your city will have regulations on this to require a certain number of spaces per employee and customer. This could get very expensive if you had to provide this yourself. With a restaurant it should already be in place.

There are exceptions to this however. If the restaurant is in a historic section of down town, it could be exempt from parking regulations that apply to the suburbs. If it is on a mass transit route, that will require fewer parking spaces as well. You will need to check with your town zoning to confirm what is currently required.

Restaurants are usually located in **high traffic** areas for the obvious reasons. Willard Marriot, before he started building hotels, was in the restaurant business. He would sit at the corner of a potential location with his wife in their car using a hand counter and click it every time a car drove by. He wanted to make sure there was adequate traffic in the area he was to build. By high traffic I mean lots of cars and foot traffic. By selecting an existing restaurant, you are usually assured that this criterion is already met.

Finally, and this is a big one, restaurants have already gone through all the **zoning** hassles to be able to serve food and probably alcohol. That means that all you are doing in most cases is what is called a "continuing use". That is, you are not changing the use from a hair salon to a restaurant. The use has already been approved for food service. I say most cases because your local zoning codes may be have something different for breweries as you are manufacturing as well as serving food and drink. But, "continuing use" can be a very large free pass. When it is a change of use situation, all sorts of expensive upgrades can be triggered. By going with a restaurant you may avoid many extra expenses.

If you start a project that is not an existing restaurant, the first thing you need to do is check with zoning to see if what you are planning can be done in that location. This will also necessitate a planning review and this takes time. By taking over an existing restaurant you are not only saving money on all the things I have already mentioned, you are also saving a whole lot of time and hassle dealing with your city.

If your town has never had to deal with a brewery before and has "no clue" as how to deal with it, you may want to contact city officials in other towns to get their input. You can relay this to your town's officials to help ease their worries. They will appreciate it if you are working with them and demonstrating that this is not new and has been done many times before.

Former KFC Turned Busy Brewpub

HOW TO FIND RESTAURANT LOCATIONS

Rent A Restaurant

The least expensive way to go is to simply find a restaurant that is for lease. As I mentioned previously, we rented a restaurant in Santa Fe, NM that the previous owners had spent $800,000 to build. It didn't work for them and came up for rent. We took it over and with a very modest expense did a re-model and opened it back up. With such little capital investment our overhead remained small giving us the breathing room to grow, and as I said earlier, over twenty-five years later that restaurant is still there.

If you have a very limited budget, your number one priority is to find a restaurant that is just for lease. I don't think I have found a town yet that doesn't have at least one. Like I said, they are always going out of business so your chances are pretty good.

The first thing I do is to drive the areas I think would be a good location for a brewpub. Someone from out of town might think one location is good, but you as a local, will know which areas are dead at night, have a bad reputation, or awkward traffic patterns. So start your search out by cruising areas you think are good. Make a note of what restaurants are in those locations and how you feel their business is doing. If there is a restaurant that looks like it has no business, keep that location in mind as it may come up for lease in the future.

Check www.craigslist.org and look under the office/ commercial section and type a search for restaurants. In the business section do the same thing. You can also check the classifieds section of your local newspaper under commercial for lease, or business opportunities.

I like to also check on Craigslist under the section For Sale, then Business. I refine it further by searching for Restaurant. In a large city you should find that quite a few pop up. In a small town only occasionally will you see something. I still like to check this where I live just to see if anything comes up.

Buy A Restaurant

If you are having trouble finding a restaurant that is for lease, you can go to restaurants that look like they might not have a thriving business and offer to buy them. Don't be too shy to ask. If anything, it is seen as a compliment to the owner, and you may be surprised that most will say that yes, for the right price, it is for sale.

When buying a business, it is not uncommon to put 20% down and pay the balance over time that the owner of the business finances. That saves you from having to go to a bank. While it is true you are buying some "blue sky" (business reputation rather than hard assets), you are also buying the restaurants leasehold improvements, plus all the kitchen equipment, and countless small items that you would have to buy anyway, such as office equipment, refrigerators, bar equipment, etc.

Things to consider when buying an existing restaurant include the age of the equipment you are buying, how old the restaurant is (negating the advantage of things being up to code like handicap restrooms), and what type of lease is in place that you could be taking over.

Another restaurant I did with my old partners was in Albuquerque. We wanted to build an Italian restaurant and the best location I found was an existing restaurant that wasn't doing too well right on Central Avenue close to the University of New Mexico.

We wound up buying the restaurant for way too much money but the location was so good we went for it anyway. Basically our knowledge of the location outweighed the cost consideration of the purchase price. Total cost to buy the existing space, totally remodel it and get open was a little over $300,000. That was a lot of money back in December 1987. As of this writing in 2014, Scalo Northern Italian Grill is still one of the most popular restaurants in that growing town.

Buying a restaurant can be a good option. In the end, you need to weigh the advantages of going this route and just building your brewpub in a space that you could lease that has never been a restaurant. Compare the numbers of overall costs for buying an existing restaurant rather than building one from scratch. That knowledge and your own gut feeling about which would be better will rule the day.

Building Your Brewpub

Sometimes none of this is appealing and you may want to start fresh with a great space that has never been a restaurant before. Go with your instincts. If you are involved throughout the process, you can finish on time and on budget. Should you choose to lease a space you have the right to ask the landlord to contribute some money for a portion of the improvement costs. Landlords are not always opposed to this because it improves their building.

When building from scratch I like to refer to the builders' triangle. Each side represents either Fast, Cheap, or Right. You can have any two of the sides, but not all three. So in other words you can do it cheap and fast, but it won't be right, or cheap and right, but it won't be fast. You get the idea.

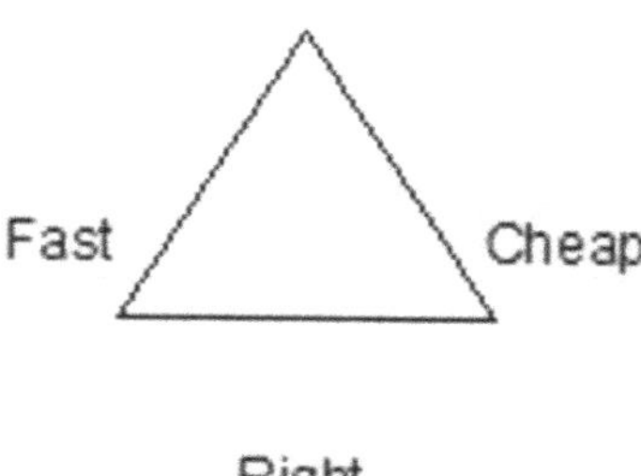

Leasing a Location for New Construction

If it is new construction, it is common for the landlord to give you a certain amount of money for the improvements. This includes expensive items like bathrooms. They may even be willing to do a complete build-out, so long as they know they will be getting their money back through lease payments. If the landlord doesn't have the cash to put into the project, you can ask them if they will abate the equivalent amount in rent over the period of the lease. At a minimum, it never hurts to ask the landlord not to charge you rent while you are under construction.

Purchasing a Location for New Construction

If you are in the position and can buy the location, talk to your lawyer and accountant about this. They may recommend that you create a separate company to own the building and lease it out to yourself. It makes a lot of sense tax-wise to do this. If the building is of historic value, it may be eligible for low interest improvement loans. The biggest plus in owning your own building is that all your improvements you are doing will go into something you own. Thereby, increasing the value of your assets.

At Colorado Boy, our current brewery, we bought our building.

Since it had never been a restaurant before I knew we would be spending a lot of money to turn it into a brewery. It made financial sense for us to purchase the building. We also got a great deal on the purchase price.

We began by creating a Limited Liability Company (LLC) to buy the building. Next we formed a corporation for the business. The corporation would build out the space and rent from the LLC. We gained the advantage of being able to control the rent. And we set it up so that the rent was lower in the beginning when business was in its infancy and growing. We then could step up rent as business increased. Colorado Boy, the corporation, improves the building making it more valuable and writes off the expenses associated with the leasehold improvements. Thus passing along to us the tax savings. Colorado Boy is a Sub-S Corporation, which allows for the pass-through of profits and losses. If we ever decided to sell Colorado Boy, we could keep the real estate and continue to rent to the brewery.

When you decide to purchase a building for your business you are entering into two separate deals. One is the real estate deal. This involves forming a separate company as I mentioned above. The other is the brewery business you are opening. Many people get hung up on the concept and think of purchasing a building and building a brewery as one deal. It is great if you can do both, but works just fine if you can only rent a building for your brewery.

To date, I have owned six breweries and in only two cases did I own the property. The others were leased. They all however were good deals because we were in business and they were profitable. There is no one-way to do this. It is wide open as far as how you structure your brewery. You just have to be open to all the possibilities.

Chapter 3

BUSINESS SET-UP

It is time now to set up you company so you have an entity to enter into contracts, sign leases, set up a bank account and file for your brewery permits. Now **I am not a lawyer**, nor do I play one on TV, but here are some things to consider before you meet with a lawyer to formally set up your company.

Four Types of Companies

If you are going to be in business you must first decide what form of business is best for you. For best results, this will involve meeting with your lawyer and accountant. Basically, there are four types of companies you can form in the U.S. and three in Canada.

- Corporation – mostly divided into two types, “C” and “S”
- Sole Proprietorship
- Partnership – general or limited
- Limited Liability Company – referred to as an L.L.C. (U.S. only)

Corporation

A corporation appears impressive. This is when you get to put those three letters after your business name like, Bill's Brewery, Inc. There is a lot to be said for choosing to become a corporation. The basic idea is that when you create a corporation, you are creating an entity unto itself.

The positive reasons for this concern liability. Bill's Brewery, Inc. owns the business, not Bill. Bill just owns the stock in the corporation. With this business structure, if someone decides to sue Bill's Brewery, Inc., they are suing the company, not the owner. The lawsuit does not "pass through" the corporation to Bill, possibly taking everything Bill owns. By protecting Bill from being sued, the corporation allows him to avoid bankruptcy if his company cannot pay its settlement costs. Remember this term, "pass through"; it will be discussed in further detail later on.

Of course, it is not as simple as all this, your lawyer can explain this in greater detail. Your lawyer will also explain the difference between a "C" corporation, which does not allow any pass through profits or losses onto your personal taxes, and an "S" corporation, which does.

In Canada, the corporation offers the same liability protections as its U.S. counterpart. Canada also offers a better tax rate on your first $200,000 of income.

As a side note I have been told by accountants that corporations are audited by the IRS less than Limited Liability Companies. I don't know if that's true but it is something to consider.

Sole Proprietorship

The simplest way to go into business is to form a sole proprietorship or a partnership. These are essentially the same in the

U.S. and Canada. All it takes is going through a simple licensing process. All you need to do is register with your state and with the IRS receiving a tax identification number.

Partnership

If you choose a partnership, you will want to make some agreements with your partner(s) that will cover essential details. These details could include compensation, raising capital, admission of new partners, hours expected to work, and most importantly how one of you can leave the partnership. All your profits and losses are passed through to your own tax reporting. If the company loses money, you can show the losses against any income you have personally. Conversely, any profits the company has will pass through to you and be taxed at your tax bracket. Also, all the liability of the company can pass through to you as well. If someone slips and falls in your brewery and decides to sue, they will be suing you. Don't let this scare you though. That's why you have insurance.

Limited Liability Company (L.L.C.)

There is another kind of business in the U.S. that you can form called a Limited Liability Company, or L.L.C. What is nice about the L.L.C. is that it does offer the same liability protection of a corporation, yet has the pass through tax benefits of a sole proprietorship or partnership without having to issue stock as in a corporation. This allows you to pass through the profits or losses to your own tax liability, which may save you money.

L.L.C.'s are usually pretty inexpensive to form as well. You still want to have similar agreements for the partners that you would have in a partnership mentioned above.

Hiring a Lawyer & Accountant

To help you understand all of this, you need to hire a lawyer and an accountant.

Your lawyer should be a corporate lawyer, not one who defends or sues. The lawyer will know how to set up your business in the best way to protect you from litigation. For example if a customer slips and falls in your brewery, the way your business is set up may help protect you personally from being named in any lawsuit that may result from an injury. A lawyer will also know how to work with accountants so that your business structure makes the most legal and financial sense.

A lawyer will not only recommend what type of business to set up, (i.e. corporation or L.L.C.) but how to include special provisions in your organization such as buy-sell agreements between you and your partners. You will also be guided to set up insurance should you die or become disabled. The insurance would fund the company to pay your heirs or pay a salary for someone to take your place if you are unable to work. It can get pretty complicated which is why you good legal advice.

When you are looking for an accountant, try to find one who has some experience in the restaurant business. This means that they should have other clients who own restaurants. You don't want to be their test client, as all businesses are different. Ask them if they have any other restaurant clients, and if they do, are they successful restaurants?

There are certain services you will need from your accountant. Besides doing your year-end and quarterly taxes, they should also provide you with a monthly profit and loss statement, or P&L. This is optional however, as you can produce your own P&L's using Quickbooks, or Peachtree Accounting software.

With your monthly profit and loss statement, they will also give you a schedule of what taxes need to be paid and when. You can do many of these things yourself depending on your comfort level, but on some things it is better to pay the experts leaving you to concentrate on your business.

Think of it this way. When setting up your company, you are going into competition with other businesses. It only makes sense to assemble the best team you can if you are going to succeed. There are plenty of places where you can save money, but good legal and accounting representation is not the area to scrimp on. If you are seriously going to do this you want a solid foundation in which to build your company. This is a good start.

Tax I.D.'s

In order to do business you must have a Federal Tax I.D. number and a State Tax I.D. number. For the Federal I.D. the simplest way is to go to irs.gov and look under business. There you will see the link to starting your own business. You can apply for your tax I.D. number on line.

For your state number you will need to contact the Secretary of State for your particular state. These days most of this can be done online.

Once you have your state and federal numbers, the government will send you several items you will need. This will include employee information, how to pay taxes online, tax coupon booklets and more.

Keep tax ID numbers with you as you are building your brewery, because you will be asked for them as you fill various applications out.

Bank Account

When you set up your company with your lawyer, she will probably suggest you put a minimum amount of money into the company to fund it. This could be as little as $2,000. This is the money you are buying your stock with, if you are setting up a corporation. Basically the IRS wants to know you are serious about starting a business and that you have contributed some of your own money.

The new company needs a place to hold and distribute funds so of course you need to set up a bank account. If you are using Quickbooks, you can order checks through them, or through your bank. If you get computer checks, get the kind that has one check on a page with two receipts. The check and one receipt goes with the bill you are paying, the third, is attached to the actual bill that you keep for your records.

If you do not have an address yet for your brewery, you can use your home address for the bank account. It is not a bad thing to have your bank statements arrive at your home rather than the business location. Eventually you can change your address to suit your needs.

To set up your bank account, you will need to give them your federal tax I.D. number, and your articles of incorporation if that is your business entity.

Accounting Software

The simplest choice is Quickbooks. It is cheap and easy to use. Accountants are all familiar with it because most of their clients use it. Most accountants prefer software like Peachtree, because once you make an entry you cannot change it, which is exactly why I don't like it. Accountants may not make mistakes but you will, and it is nice if you can go back and correct them.

Once you get your Quickbooks package you can order your checks and check envelopes through them as I just mentioned. You should also get a check endorsement stamp as well for the checks you will be receiving, especially if you have wholesale accounts.

You can also order a payroll module for your Quickbooks. This will allow you to do your own payroll and will be set up for all your current tax rates and reporting.

Lastly get your accountant or a bookkeeper to set up your Quickbooks with a chart of accounts to keep track of your equipment purchases. This will get you started in the right direction and make it easier to figure it all out come tax time.

Hire A Bookkeeper

You will be doing your daily books, which include accounts payable and receivable, payroll, and your daily sales recording. I suggest using a bookkeeper to come in once a month to take care of all your tax payments and recording. Again, let the pros do this so you can concentrate on running your business. I have tried numerous times to pay the many different taxes for myself and I always make mistakes. For the cost of $100 per month it is all done accurately and professionally and I don't have to worry about it. You shouldn't either.

Chapter 4

ACQUIRE YOUR BUILDING

At this point, you have created a company, funded it, opened a bank account, and set up your Quickbooks to track everything. You also have found a location that suits you and tied it up for a bit with a letter of intent, which is a simple letter you give the landlord saying that you intend to lease the space if it meets certain expectations. Now it is time to move on the space and get going. Here are a few last steps before you actually sign the lease, close on your contract to purchase or rent.

Brewery Design

The first order of business, once you have found an existing restaurant for lease, is to figure out the best place to put the brewery. Generally speaking you should be fine with about 150 sq. ft. for the brew-house and fermentation, and another 150 to 200 sq. ft. for the conditioning room. That of course depends on the type and size of the equipment you use.

Typically a restaurant is divided in half with the front being the dining room, and the back the kitchen. So you know you will be putting the brewery in the back of your space as that is where the floor drains are. This also creates easier access for removing grain and taking deliveries. Note: this is not always the case. Depending on the look of the building and your judgment, you may want to put the brewery, or at least the brew-house, right by the front door.

If the brewery is going to be in the kitchen area, position the conditioning tanks as close to the dining area as you can. Ideally they would be directly behind the bar so that there can be a direct line from the tanks to the taps. If that is the case, there should be some way for the customer to view the tanks. You can place a window or open area for the brew-house possibly with a dividing wall.

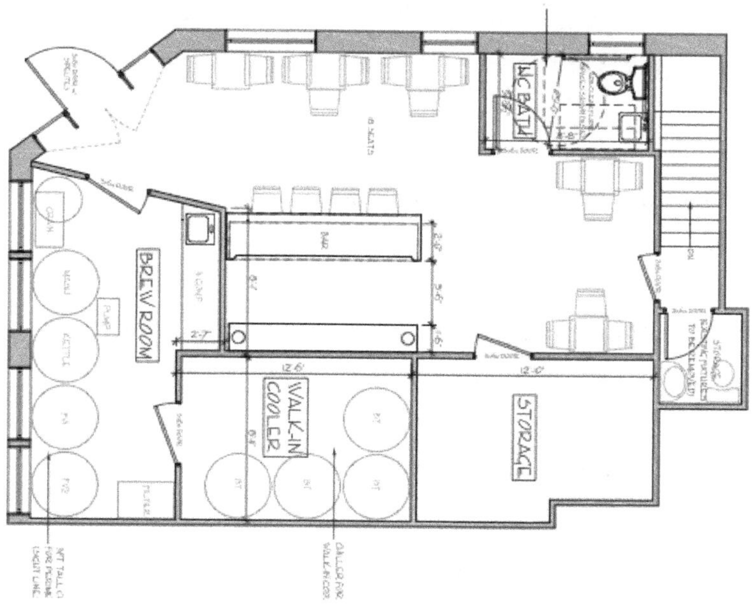

Colorado Boy's Original Plans

At Colorado Boy there is a 5 ft. high wall that separates the brew-house from the bar area. This arrangement was fine with our local building department, but you need to check with your local officials to see if that would work for you. Keep in mind however that a full wall will keep the grain dust, heat and humidity out of the dining room. To accomplish this at Colorado Boy we would only have to add glass from the top of the wall to the ceiling. Sometimes the building department may require a wire mesh glass instead of clear. We had to do that in a brewery I built in Albuquerque. The building department doesn't understand the brewing process and thinks the brew kettle will blow up.

As you can see by the diagram, Colorado Boy is a very tiny brewery of about 1,200 sq. ft. This includes a 200 sq. ft. basement where a small office, and grain storage is located. Most restaurants you find for lease or sale will be at least this big. Since Ridgway only has 800 residents, a small brewery with 20 seats works out fine. If I were to build a similar style brewery in a larger town, I would try to fit in at least 50 seats.

Since the original plans were made, Colorado Boy has added a kitchen into the storage space, extended the bar and put a bench seat along the window area. With that, Colorado Boy only needs two bartenders and two cooks to handle a standing room only crowd. This is a key point. By keeping the overhead as low as possible, a good profit can be made by even a small brewery.

Building Inspector Walk-Through

Once you have drawn up a rough diagram of how your pub will be set-up, contact your local building inspector and ask them if they could do a walk-through of your space. Get their feedback on what you are planning to do. There are two great advantages to this:

#1. They can give you a heads up if they see any potential problems you may encounter. Two examples could be the necessity of a sprinkler system, or providing adequate access for venting your equipment.

#2. They will appreciate that you are involving them at the beginning. Many people approach the building department in their town as adversaries and the whole project becomes a struggle. If your building inspector knows that you are trying to do the right thing, as evidenced by involving their input right from the start, they are more likely to help coach you in the process. This will make your process much smoother and likely save you money.

Do The Deal

If the building inspector sees no problems, the zoning is correct, and you have funding in place, you are now ready to sign your lease or close on purchasing your property. Everything you have done so far has gotten you to the starting block and now you are ready to run.

Chapter 5

LICENSING

Every business deals with licenses and laws particular to its own industry, and this is especially true with breweries. The licenses required to run a brewpub or microbrewery are different according to where you do business. What is the same everywhere are the three levels of licenses:

1.Federal
2.State
3.Local

U.S. Brewers Permits

In the U.S. there is one basic permit that is issued by the federal government to manufacture beer. This used to be handled by the Bureau of Alcohol, Tobacco and Firearms, or by the acronym ATF. A new division of the ATF was formed called the Alcohol and Tobacco Tax and Trade Bureau, or the TTB, which now handles the brewers' permits.

There is no fee for the permit, but there is an application that must be filled out and sent in duplicate. Go to www.ttb.gov/

applications/brewery_brewpub_packet.shtml to see the list of forms you need to download and fill out.

It is now also possible to fill out the forms and submit them online. Brewers I have spoken to who have done this have reported that it took less time than the four to five months it used to take. One of my students recently (2012) told me it took him only 24 days!

But whether you fill the forms out online or by mail they can still be a little confusing. Here is a brief description of each one.

Brewers Notice

This is the first form to fill out. When it asks for a serial number just write 1, as this is your first notice to them. After that it is pretty straightforward until you get to the signing authority. This is just the title of the officers or managers. List the person's name and title. For the next section for brewpubs, just initial the boxes and list what size serving vessels you will have, such as 7 BBL. If you are not planning on not serving food, then skip that section. You are considered a brew put only if you serve food. Next are the lists of attachments you must provide or forms found at the above website.

Articles of Incorporation

If you are a corporation or an L.L.C. your lawyer provided you with articles of incorporation. You must include a copy of them with your application.

Trade Name Registration

This is only if your state requires you to register your name. My state of Colorado does, so I include a copy of the registration obtained from the Secretary of State's web site.

Power of Attorney

This is a very simple form showing who has authority in your brewery to sign forms and reports for the TTB.

Diagram

This is the plat of the area where your brewery is located. It may show your whole block. You will outline your brewery space and be sure that it shows the dimensions of the brewery. You can get a copy of this from your county assessor.

Legal Description of the Brewery

Your county assessor will give you the legal description of the location of your brewery. This is just a simple paragraph with the description on a piece of paper.

Here is ours: Unit 2, Drashan Condominiums, according to the recorded plat filed January 23, 2007 at reception No. 194017, and the declaration recorded January, 2007 at reception No. 19321, as amended from time to time, Town of Ridgway, County of Ouray, State of Colorado. Also known as street number 602 Clinton Street Ridgway, CO 81432

Supplemental Information of Water Quality

Here is an example of ours at Colorado Boy. Note that the serial number is the form number for the Brewers Notice.

OMB No.1513-0023 (08/31/2011)

DEPARTMENT OF THE TREASURY
ALCOHOL AND TOBACCO TAX AND TRADE BUREAU

SUPPLEMENTAL INFORMATION ON WATER QUALITY CONSIDERATIONS UNDER 33 U.S.C. 1341(a)

INSTRUCTIONS

1. **COMPLETION.** Answer all items in sufficient detail if applicable to your activity. If necessary, continue on a separate sheet. Your answers are evaluated to determine if certification or waiver by the applicable State Water Quality Agency is required under Section 21 of the Federal Water Pollution Control Act (33 U.S.C. 1341(a)).

2. **FILING.** Submit an original and one copy of this form with the related application or other document, to the Director, National Revenue Center, 550 Main St, Ste 8002, Cincinnati, Ohio 45202-5215. This form must be completed and submitted even though three copies of the required certification or waiver have been sent to the Director, National Revenue Center or are attached to this form.

3. **DISPOSITION.** After final action taken on the related application or other document, the copy of this form will be returned to the applicant.

APPLICATION RELATED TO THIS RIDER

1. FORM NUMBER	2. APPLICATION DATE	3. SERIAL NUMBER
	xx/xx/xxxx	TTB F 5130.10

4. NAME AND PRINCIPAL BUSINESS ADDRESS OF APPLICANT (Number, street, city, county, State, and ZIP code)	5. PLANT ADDRESS (If different from address in item 4)

6. DESCRIBE ACTIVITY TO BE CONDUCTED IN WHICH THE ALCOHOL AND TOBACCO TAX AND TRADE BUREAU HAS AN INTEREST.
Brewing Beer

7. DESCRIBE ANY DIRECT OR INDIRECT DISCHARGE INTO NAVIGABLE WATERS WHICH MAY RESULT FROM THE CONDUCT OF THE ACTIVITY DESCRIBED IN ITEM 6, INCLUDING THE BIOLOGICAL, CHEMICAL, THERMAL, OR OTHER CHARACTERISTIC OF THE DISCHARGE AND THE LOCATIONS AT WHICH SUCH DISCHARGE MAY ENTER NAVIGABLE WATERS.
Nothing will be discharged into navigable waters.

8. GIVE THE DATE OR DATES ON WHICH THE ACTIVITY WILL BEGIN AND END, IF KNOWN, AND ON WHICH THE DISCHARGE WILL TAKE PLACE.
xx/xx/xxxx

9. DESCRIBE THE METHODS AND MEANS USED OR TO BE USED TO MONITOR THE QUALITY AND CHARACTERISTICS OF THE DISCHARGE AND THE OPERATION OF EQUIPMENT OR FACILITIES EMPLOYED IN THE TREATMENT OR CONTROL OF WASTES OR OTHER EFFLUENTS.
City of Ridgway, Colorado has installed a valve in-line in the sewer system allowing them to take samples of brewery efluent for analysis.

I certify that I have examined this rider and, to the best of my knowledge and belief, it is true, correct, and complete and that copies of this rider may be furnished to the applicable State Water Quality Agency and the Regional Administrator, Environmental Protection Agency.

10. APPLICANT	11. BY (Signature and title)

TTB F 5000.30 (10/2008)

Personal Questionnaire

Hopefully you are not like me and have not moved several times, because on this form, you have to list all your residences for the last ten years. You must also include everywhere you have worked.

By-Laws

You will have this with your corporate documents. Just include a copy with your packet upon submission.

Partnership Agreement

This is in place of your By-Laws if you are not a corporation or L.L.C. but rather a Partnership or Sole-Proprietorship. It's similar and something your lawyer will write up.

Environmental Information

This is similar to the Supplemental Information On Water Quality form above. Here is what we filled in for our pub.

OMB No. 1513-0023 (08/31/2011)

DEPARTMENT OF THE TREASURY
ALCOHOL AND TOBACCO TAX AND TRADE BUREAU (TTB)

ENVIRONMENTAL INFORMATION

INSTRUCTIONS

1. **COMPLETION.** Answer all items in sufficient detail or as not applicable to your activity. The information on all items should relate to the activity in which the Bureau has an interest. If additional space is required for any item, please attach a separate sheet identified by the item number of this form. Your answers are evaluated by the Bureau to determine whether the activity will have a significant effect on the environment. If TTB F 5000.30, Supplemental Information on Water Quality Considerations - Under 33 U.S.C. 1341(a), is also being submitted for your activity, you may make reference to any relevant information given on TTB F 5000.30 for items 6 and 7 of this form.

2. **FILING.** Submit an original and one copy of this form to the Director, National Revenue Center, 550 Main St, Ste 8002, Cincinnati, OH 45202-5215.

3. **DISPOSITION.** After final action taken on the related application or other document, the copy of this form will be returned to the applicant.

1. Name and Principal Business Address of Applicant	2. Description of Activity in which Alcohol and Tobacco Tax and Trade Bureau has an interest	3. Number of Employees
Colorado Boy Brewing Co. Inc. 602 Clinton St. Ridgway, CO 81432	Brewery	

4. Location Where Activity is to be Conducted *(Be specific, Number, Street, City, State, ZIP Code; describe locations of buildings and outside equipment and their situation relative to surrounding environment including other structures, land use, lakes, streams, roads, railroad facilities, etc. Maps, photos, or drawings may be provided.)*

602 Clinton St. Ridgway, CO 81432. Approximately one mile west from the Uncompadre River, and three miles south of the Ridgway reservoir.

5. Heat and Power:

A. Describe types of heat and power to be used and their sources. If they are to be produced in connection with the proposed activity, estimate type and quantity of fuel to be used for each purpose. *(Example: 40 tons/yr. anthracite coal for heat, 20 million cu.-ft./yr. natural for power generating.)*

Electricity is provided by San Miguel Power Company. Gas for heat and brewing is provided by Source Gas Company, both local utilities.

B. Describe any air pollution control equipment proposed for use in connection with fuel burning equipment, boilers, or smokestacks.

None will be used.

6. Solid Waste:

A. Describe amount and composition of all solid waste to be generated.

Approximately 400 pounds spent grain per week.
Approximately 7 pounds of spent hops per week.

B. Discuss proposed methods of disposal *(Incineration, open burning, landfill, government or commercial garbage collection, etc.)* Specify whether on-site or off-site.

Spent grain to be fed to local cattle.
Spent hops turn to sludge and are disposed of through drain pipes to city sewer.

C. Describe any air pollution control equipment proposed for use in connection with any incinerators.

None.

TTB F 5000.29 (10/2008)

Diagram For Brewpub

Submit a drawing of your layout that shows dimensions, the tasting room, and all the beer tanks in their proper place. Highlight the area around the brew house, fermentation, and conditioning room to identify all brewing operations. Then write on the diagram which is the tasting area, and which is the brewing operation.

Statement Describing Security For The Brewery

This can be just a simple paragraph explaining that the beer tanks that hold the finished beer are in a lockable walk-in cooler. Also, state that the entire premise is to be locked when not open to the public and that you has an alarm system installed. Really, this only needs to be a paragraph.

Bond

You are also required to secure a bond that is sufficient to cover any taxes due. The minimum bond is $1,000.00, and you have two choices. First is a **Surety Bond**. This is obtained from an insurance agent (there is a list on the TTB web site). The agency will charge you $100.00 per year for a $1,000.00 bond.

I prefer however to just fill out the **Collateral Bond** form and send them a certified check for $1,000.00 that they will hold as long as you are in business. It will save you $100.00 per year, which is more than you could make if your $1,000.00 were in the bank.

Once all the paper work has been completed, you send it in and it will take anywhere from four to five months for the application process to be completed. However, if you apply online, it could take less time. It is best to be prepared in your timeline for the longer period. The TTB will get back to you with questions and undoubtedly there will be some.

When all is completed, an agent will come out and inspect your operation to make sure it is as you mapped it out. In my last brewery, the agent also helped fill out some small corrections in the application while she was there. In all cases I've experienced only very helpful agents.

State Licenses

Getting a brewers license from your state varies from state to state. Here in Colorado it is very simple and takes about three months. In New Mexico, just the next state south, the process takes four months.

Unfortunately, with fifty states there are fifty different rules that apply to obtaining a beer-manufacturing license. Listed in the index section are the web site addresses for each state so that you can easily check out the particular requirements for your state.

Local Licensing

Local licensing usually has to do with zoning. In other words, will the city or county allow beer manufacturing in your location?

The first step in looking for a location for your brewery involves checking with your city or county government to see if they allow brewpubs or microbreweries where you are thinking of placing one. To find out, go to your local government and ask.

The last brewery I opened was in downtown Palisade, Colorado. The location was zoned as B-1, which means light commercial activity. Luckily for me about 10 years previously they amended the B-1 to allow wineries (there are a lot in Palisade) and since they allowed wineries, they ultimately were willing to include microbreweries. When

I went to the city to ask them if it was OK to put the brewery in this zone, they thought it didn't meet the requirement. Upon closer look at the zoning regulations they found that it was.

In many states obtaining a brewers license begins with your local authority. The whole process is handled through the city. After their local city council has approved the project, the application is then forwarded to the state. Your city or county clerk will be able to tell you the process.

Canadian Brewers Permits

To brew beer in Canada only requires licenses issued by the provinces with zoning permission from the local city or town. Canada is a very beer friendly country and home of North Americas oldest continuously operating brewery (Molson's).

Each province has its own unique application process but they are all similar to this:

- Fill out a manufacturer's license application.
- Fill out a personal history and consent to search form.
- Obtain written confirmation from local zoning authorities.
- Collect any other required documentation.
- Pay the license fee (different in each province).
- Send the packet in.

Costs vary, but generally there is an application fee of $550 and a license fee around $550 To $1,500. These fees are paid every year and you must re-apply every year also. A list of web sites for Canadian Provinces is located in the index in the back of this book.

STEP 2

BUILD IT

Chapter 6

CONSTRUCTION

Many of the contractors we used were people we knew. The person or company you choose to build your brewery will determine when you open and how much money you spend. Here are some things to look for when picking your contractor.

Of course, you may not be using a contractor at all (if your town will let you), but rather just you and your buddies helping you for free beer (my preference), but if that is not the case, the following section may be helpful if you have never built anything commercial before.

Collect Three Bids

If it is possible, try to get at least three bids. When doing this, it is important to compare apples to apples. In other words, make sure that your bids are from the same set of plans. If you have hired an architect, you will be handing out copies of duplicate plans for the contractors to bid on. If you are just remodeling an existing restaurant space, you have to be very careful when you explain what you want done to the contractor. You will need to repeat the exact same instructions to all the other contractors.

If you are not careful, one contractor will suggest a better way of doing something in their bid, and then the next contractor will have a different way of doing something else. In the end, you will have three different bids on three different projects. Stick to your initial plan at least for comparison. You can always go back and change things later once you decide which contractor you want to use.

Contractor References

When getting your bids together, be sure to ask each contractor for a list of references. Most importantly, call all the references! This is one of your best resources for discovering the true qualities of the contractors. When checking references, ask if you can go see the work that the contractor has done. If you don't know that much about how things are put together, at least you will have the satisfaction of actually seeing something that was built by the contractor. Usually you can get a sense of the quality of the work. When talking to the references make a list of questions to ask each of them. Ask these same questions of each reference. Here are some ideas:

- Was the work finished on time and on budget?
- Did the contractor do everything they said they would do?
- Did the workers clean up at the end of the day?
- Were there many change orders?
- Were the contractor and crew boss pleasant to work with?
- Would you work with them again?

The more references you talk to, the better the over-all impression you will have of the contractor. If the bids are close, this is important when deciding who will get the job.

Change Orders

Cost is not the only important consideration when picking a contractor. When checking references, you can find out how often there were change orders.

A change order is something extra you ask for, or the contractor suggests. This is work that is done during the building process. Sometimes a contractor will bid low, knowing that they can make up the money by insisting on change orders. Remember the change orders were not bid on. They can be priced at a premium.

So when the contractor suggests a change order because he "didn't really know until they got into the walls," you need to take a moment to examine all the alternatives. If you readily agree to the change order, keep track of them so the final bill does not surprise you.

Most likely it will be you who wants to change things once you get started. Again, all the more reason to be sure of your plans before you begin the building project.

With most of our restaurants and breweries, I laid out the floor plan before I give it to the architect. I use masking tape to outline all the tables, chairs and counter tops on the bare floor. Next, I sit on a large ladder in the middle of the room so I can imagine the traffic. I feel it is important to "see it". When the restaurant is built, it will look just as I had imagined it. No surprises - hopefully.

Once you have hired your contractor, request a copy of their contractor's license, and insurance coverage for your file. They are required to have liability insurance and workman's compensation insurance.

Spending Time on the Job Site

Spend as much time on the job site as you can. Be a part of the crew when it comes time to clean up at the end of the day. Bring in donuts and coffee and get to know the crew boss and workers. The more they get to know you, the more they will want to see you succeed and be less likely to take advantage of your check book. It's not to say they would, but it just makes me feel better if the workers don't think of me as a nameless rich corporation.

The Walk Through

As the great day approaches and the building nearly finished, you will do a walk through with your contractor and develop a punch list. This is a list that has all the small items that still need to be finished, fixed, or cleaned up. Once everything on the list is done, then the contractor gets his final check.

Contractor Payments

For small jobs, contractors like to be paid half up front. On larger jobs, that figure can go down to 20% and then payments can be made weekly, semi-monthly, or monthly until the project is completed. It is very rare that a construction company will hold off billing until the project is finished.

By the end of the project, you will hopefully be pretty close to all the people who helped you. It is a good idea to invite them to your opening. These are your first goodwill ambassadors who will let the community know about you. It is time to start thinking of everyone as a potential customer.

TIP: If you are home brewing, set up a keg and tap it at the end of the day, or end of the week. You can imagine how the crew will love working on your project!

Chapter 7

FRANKENBREW

You have your company and your capitol. You have signed your lease or bought your building, checked with zoning and building inspectors and have submitted to the building department for a building permit. All your liquor license applications are in the works, so now you need to start accumulating equipment.

Brewing System Size

I like the "nano-breweries" that are springing up across America these days. But, it just doesn't make sense to have a production capacity too small. I have seen small breweries open in towns bigger than our own, only to find that they have to spend all their time brewing just to keep up.

It takes about the same time to brew 1 barrel as it does to make 7. I would rather brew once or twice a week and have all that extra time to do other things like enjoy my life rather than have to brew every day and still have trouble keeping my taps full.

That being said, I have a lot of respect for Tim Myers at Strange Brewing in Denver, Colorado. After being laid off at Rocky Mountain News when they shut down, he used his home brew 20-gallon set up and opened up Strange Brewing. He would have liked to have a seven-barrel system but couldn't afford it. So he brewed almost every day for a year. By the end of that time he had paid off all his initial investment and managed to buy a used seven-barrel system. Now he is well on his way to a bright beer future.

So though you may be planning a brewery as small as Colorado Boy, I would suggest a system of at least 5 barrels, and preferably 7. A minimum set up would have the following:

- Brew Kettle
- Mash Tun
- One Fermenter
- Three Serving Tanks

This would allow you to brew once a week and have about 5 or 6 beers on tap, using kegs and serving vessels in combination. If you are busy, you will have trouble keeping up, as your maximum capacity would be 14 kegs per week. If you do any volume in growler sales, that can eat into your beer supply quite quickly. We sell almost a keg's worth of growlers every day, so you can see how a one-barrel system just wouldn't do.

By adding a second fermenter you can double your production with only the additional cost of one tank. Everything else is in place, so the return on investment is assured. However, once you are brewing twice in a seven-day period, you will feel the pressure to move beer out of your serving tanks to make room for your new beer from the fermenters. At this point it would make sense to add one or two serving tanks. These cost less and will enable you to serve out of them longer as compared to serving from kegs. It takes more labor and chemicals to clean kegs.

Here we see a better system with pretty much the same footprint:

- Brew Kettle
- Mash Tun
- Two Fermenters
- Five Serving Tanks.

The best system for a small brewery allows for much more flexibility in schedules, types of beer brewed, and beers on tap. Be aware that we are only talking about brewing ales. Small systems do not have the space to make lagers. If you add one or two more fermenters, you can possibly have a lager taking up a fermenter without hurting the production of the ales you need to have on tap. By having more serving vessels you can expand the amount of beers available. The more beers you have on tap, the slower any one will run out because the customer has more choices.

If I had the space in Colorado Boy, this would be the set up I would love to have:

- Brew Kettle
- Mash Tun
- Three or Four Fermenters
- Eight to Ten Serving Tanks

With this system I could have all the best sellers on, one or two lagers, and even some aged or experimental beers. You will find that whatever system you start with, you will constantly be expanding it and pushing it to its limits. Every brewer has a wish list.

FLOORS

One of the most talked about subjects is the type of floor for a brewery. Brewing chemicals will destroy most materials over time and everyone has what they believe is the best material.

Personally I have found that plain sealed concrete floors work the best. For a 7-barrel system a 4-inch slab is sufficient. When I had a 20-barrel system with 40-barrel tanks, there were no problems with weight or cracking using a 6-inch slab.

If you are taking over part of a kitchen space in a restaurant, chances are good that it already has a concrete floor, because of the weight of the kitchen equipment. Other flooring you may encounter might include vinyl tile on wood, or ceramic tile over wood.

If you are dealing with a wood floor, there are a couple of options. First you could put the thickest sheet of industrial grade vinyl over it and support the area from below with pillars on concrete footers. You will need an engineer to draw it up for your building department's approval. Second instead of vinyl you could pour a layer of concrete on top of the wood but would still need all the supports mentioned in the first option. Make sure that you have something that won't melt, like tile, under the brew kettle.

The third option applies if the building is old and the floor joists are sitting on the ground or close to it. You can cut the wood out exposing the dirt underneath. Then you can have your drains and all plumbing put in place, add road base to build up the floor and pour new concrete to make your brewery floor. With the option of a new floor you can slope the floor so liquid flows to the drain.

Of the six breweries I have owned, only our current Colorado Boy has floors that flow to the drain. This is because we had wood floors and did exactly as I just described. If you go this route, make sure you are there when they pour the floor and stand over the workers to make sure that they set the concrete up to actually slope to the drain. If you are not there, chances are there will be spots in the floor that are not sloped properly, leaving you to deal with that one area in the back corner where all your liquids pool, making it hard to get to with a squeegee.

If you find that your space has concrete floors already in place, you will either work the placement of the equipment around where floor drains are located, or you will have to cut in new floor drains and connect them to the existing plumbing system. This is where the squeegee becomes your friend, as you will be using it every time you brew. If this is the case, you should build up some curbing so the liquid from brewing stays in the brew house and does not flow out into the rest of the kitchen.

There are three kinds of floor drains you can choose. The first is a simple round drain, the second is a floor sink, and the third is a trench drain.

The simple floor drain is cheap and works fine as long as you have a good cover on it so brewing parts don't fall into it. If you are taking over a restaurant, you won't find this kind of drain in the kitchen, as floor sinks are more common. I don't care for floor sinks because you trip on them, and everything collects there. If you do have them, they make a stainless screen that fits inside the floor sink that will protect you from losing all your small hose clamps and gaskets that will eventually fall into them.

The best option is to add a trench drain, especially if you find you are going to be cutting the concrete anyway to add more drains. One strategically placed trench drain can take care of your entire brew house. They are more expensive but pretty slick too.

PROCESS FLOW – FROM GRAIN TO GLASS

In the old days breweries were constructed in three or four tiers. Grain was delivered to the top floor, where it was milled and flowed down the next floor to the mash and lauder-tun, and then flowed down to the kettle. From the kettle, the wort moved down a floor to the fermentation room, and from the fermentation room down a floor to the conditioning room, where it was filtered and packaged and sent out to the delivery trucks on the ground floor.

Even with your small brewery some thought should be given to the flow of the brewing process. If you want the conditioning tanks next to the bar where beer will be served, it only makes sense that the fermentation tanks would be located close by the conditioning tanks. The fermentation tanks therefore should be fairly close to the brew house to avoid long transfer hoses.

In our brewery in Salida, Colorado the building was a shotgun of a structure that was 25 feet wide by 150 feet long. All grain was stored at the back door. Moving forward was the brew- house, followed by a small room that contained the fermentation tanks. The next room forward was the conditioning room, which had 8 Grundy tanks (I will explain what a Grundy is later when we go over equipment). It would have made sense to place the bar next. However, for design purposes, we put a wood burning pizza oven next. So the bar was actually 50 feet away from the conditioning room. We used a glycol-chilled trunk line to move the beer to the bar and that worked well. All the rooms were glass on one side so customers could see the process.

The closer the tanks are to each other, the less pumping needed. Less pumping saves energy, and is gentler on the beer. If you have more than one story to work with, you may even eliminate having to use a pump, and use gravity instead. A brewery we did in Colorado

Springs had the brew house right above the fermentation room. I used a six-inch diameter piece of PVC in the brew house floor with a cap as an access point. When transferring from the kettle to the fermenter I simply ran a hose downstairs and gravity pulled the wort. Rate of flow was determined by how much I opened the valve. When the brew was finished transferring I replaced the cap on the PVC to prevent water or debris from falling down into the fermentation room.

When laying out the brewery in the empty restaurant you are going to rent or purchase, you should give a lot of thought as to how your brewing process will flow from grain to glass. It will save you a lot of headaches in the future. For example, if you have extra space, leave it blank so you can add serving-tanks as you need them. And think about how you will get tanks in and out of those rooms. Having a four-foot door could be a lifesaver.

EQUIPMENT

Let's assume this will be a 7-barrel system, so all these discussions will be sized for that. Most small breweries should do well with just 7 barrels, or 14 kegs of production per brew. You would only need to think of a larger system if you plan on packaging in bottles or cans for distribution.

There are many options for the various tanks you need for your brewery. We will go through each one and discuss the different options.

The Mash Tun

You will want a vessel that can hold around 200 gallons. You could get by with 150 gallons, but you would be limited on the gravity of your beers as you would not be able to put as much grain in. Likewise, you could use a tank that holds 300 gallons, but then you risk a mash depth that is too thin for 7 barrels, but I am getting ahead of myself.

The shape of the tank is not too important. Traditionally both cylindrical and rectangular vessels have been used. Here are two options.

For a cylindrical mash tun, I recommend you use a Grundy tank. This is a tank I will mention often in this book.

These are the cellar tanks typically used in the United Kingdom. In the 1980s, when they started arriving here, they became the true fertilizer for the growth of American craft-brewing. The reason is simple; they are cheap, and the stainless welds and finish on the inside are excellent. They hold pressure, and are light enough for two guys to pick up and move around. They also hold 7 barrels, if you fill them up to the site glasses. They come with either a top man-way or side a man-way. You can usually pick them up for around $1,000 to $1,500.

Typical Grundy Tanks

To make a mash tun out of a Grundy, you will need to cut the top off at the top weld line. Then you will need to have a stainless band welded around the top perimeter to strengthen it. To create a false bottom, you will have to have a round frame made to support a perforated stainless steel screen. Don't forget the frame needs to be stainless as well. The false bottom should sit above the bottom of the Grundy about 8 inches. You don't need a top for it, but you could make one out of Plexiglas or some other material if you choose. I found no discernable temperature drop from not having a cover on the vessel.

Grundy Mash Tun

There are also round dairy tanks and these also make excellent mash tuns. In fact they may even be better as Grundies are becoming harder to find and the dairy tanks are insulated. Most of these tanks come with tri-clamp ports already at the bottom.

Dairy Tank

The other type of mash Tun is a rectangular vessel. For these your best bet is to use a dairy style tank, commonly used for milk chilling. The dairy industry doesn't use these anymore, so they are readily available and cheap. These can be found behind barns for around $200. It is more likely that you will find them for $2,000 at companies that deal in used dairy equipment. While this may seem expensive, there is really no modification that needs to be done to the tank. In fact, you don't even need to make a false bottom.

Milk Chiller Dairy Tank

I have found that with these tanks you just need one long pipe, about 1.5 inches O.D. (outside diameter) that extends the length of the inside of the vessel. Cut slits into the pipe along the bottom, which will allow the wort through, but not the grain. The pipe can be made from stainless steel or copper. It needs to be capped on one end. The open end just gets pushed into the outlet of the tank.

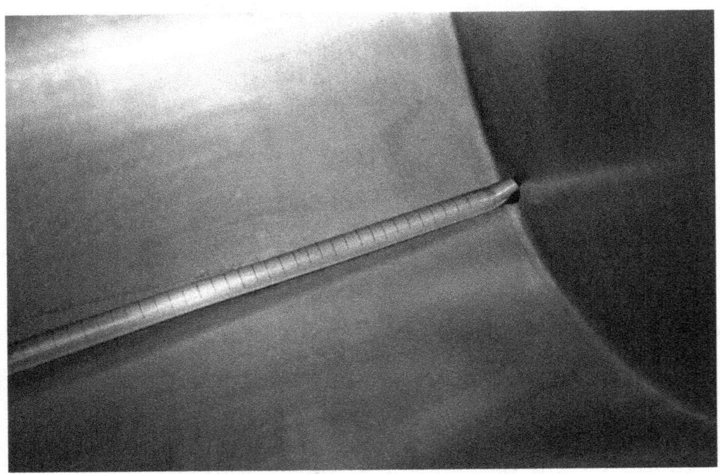

Slices cut onto one side of pipe

Pipe in place with slices facing down

When I am doing a vorlauf (recirculation of wort) from this type of false bottom, I get really clear wort almost immediately, as compared to the false bottoms that are screens. I have also seen this type of system used in a round dairy tank as well. Rather than just one single pipe, you piece together a grid or circular piece to fit in the bottom.

Our first mash tun

What is also nice about these vessels is they usually come with lids, and they are insulated. In fact they are jacketed as well, which you will see comes in handy for other uses.

No matter which of these vessels you choose, you will need to make a sparge fixture for them. A sparge fixture is simply a showerhead that allows hot sparge water (hot liquor) to flow evenly onto the mash.

In the Frankenbrew systems I have made, I usually just sweat copper tubes together in some grid or ladder shape that fits the style of mash tun I am using. Then I drill a bunch of holes in the pipes so the water showers over the mash. The latest one I made is even simpler. It is a single pipe with hack saw cuts spaced every inch. This costs about $30 in materials and about an hour to make.

Hot Liquor Tank

This vessel just holds hot water that you will need for sparging your mash. It can be any shape, and made out of almost any material, although I would recommend stainless rather than plastic.

Most commercial hot liquor tanks have an electric heating element in them. They usually sit next to the brew kettle and the mash tun, and the water from the hot liquor tank is pumped to the mash tun. Of course that is not the Frankenbrew (cheap) way.

For a 7-barrel system you should have a tank that can hold 150 to 200 gallons of water. It is beneficial if it is insulated but not that important, as I have experienced very little temperature drop in the time the water is pumped to the hot liquor tank until it is used for sparge.

If the tank sits up on racks that are higher than the mash tun, then you can gravity feed the water for sparging rather than using an extra pump.

Instead of needing a heating element in the tank, you can heat the water in your brew kettle after you have mashed-in, then transfer the water to the hot liquor tank. I will go over this when we go through the entire brew process.

Another variation of a hot liquor tank would be to use the fermentation vessel that you will be using later the same day. In this case you will need an extra pump.

To do this, you simply heat your sparge water in the brew kettle to about 180 degrees and pump it to the fermenter you will be using that day. This hot water will not hurt your clean and sanitized fermenter. When it comes time to sparge, you will pump out of the fermenter to the sparge head. It will lose some heat, which is why I heat the water to about 180 degrees, knowing that when it comes out of the sparge arm it will be about 170 degrees.

Brew Kettle

Here we get to the heart of your system. First let's talk about shape. I prefer cylindrical as opposed to rectangular. The reason for this is so you can whirlpool and more easily separate out the trub and hops from the wort at the end of your brew.

Your choices of tanks include the Grundy or any dairy process tank that fits the bill.

If you choose to use a Grundy, you will need to pick a way to heat it. For the most part you have two choices, direct flame and electric.

Direct Fired Grundy Brew Kettle

Direct flame is an excellent way to heat your brew kettle. To fit a burner under the kettle will require some modifications however.

First you will need to make a heat shield to go around the outlet and the bottom of the tank. If you don't do this, you will scorch your wort. This should be welded to the bottom of the tank so that the outlet is completely sealed off from any exposed flame. It wouldn't hurt either to add flameproof insulation inside the shield.

Next you will need to make a skirt around the bottom of the tank. This should be welded just below the bottom weld marks on the Grundy. On one side of the skirt weld in a six to eight inch ring, so that you can attach an exhaust vent. Needless to say, all your welding should be in stainless. These welds do not have to be sanitary welds, as they do not come in contact with the wort.

For the flame you must contact your local building inspector to see what they will allow. For my first one I got a 199,000 BTU burner from a commercial hot water heater (for free) and supported that under the kettle. Our local inspector required the addition of a safety switch with a heat sensor attached to the kettle, so if it got too hot it would turn the burner off.

A good commercial burner you could buy is an Economite DS24A. This runs about $800 but is an excellent burner. It is a blower type burner so you would need a 4-inch opening at the bottom of your skirt to fit this in. Your skirt would need to be closed at the bottom as well to hold the heat in. Get a plumbing contractor to install it so they can test the gas to adjust it for efficiency. They will also add a balance inlet to the gas flu outlet. As the flu heats up instead of drawing more air out of the fire box, which would affect your burner, it has a door that swings open, bringing in air from the room. This is very important for burner efficiency.

Economite DS24A

Next you will need to add two more outlets to the kettle; the first one at the bottom, just above the existing outlet and the lower weld. The second one should be one third up from the bottom and to the side. This is what you will need to do your whirlpool. These outlets should be inch and a half tri-clamp.

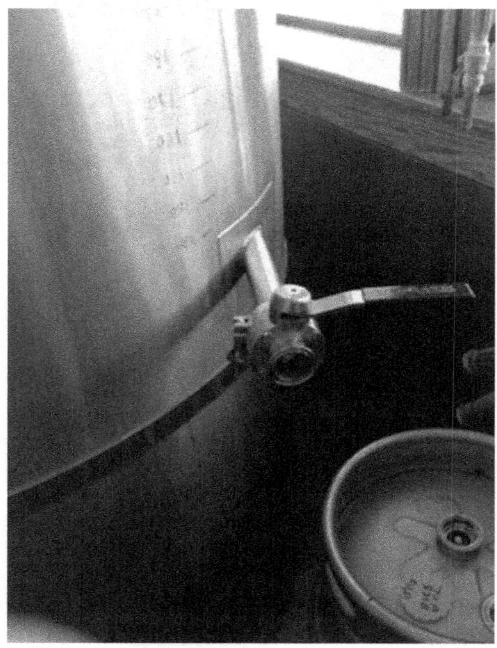

Kettle Whirl Pool

Finally, you should put another 6-inch ring in the lid of the Grundy so you can attach a steam vent. In practical terms however, I usually always leave the lid off during a brew. This way there is less chance of a boil over. If you can just vent the steam into the room, or under a kitchen style exhaust hood, you can leave the top off and do all of your hop additions from the top. However if you do use the lid, you will need one more opening in the top, just to the side of the sight glass with its own lid for adding hops.

Now if you go electric, you will still need to do all the additions to the brew kettle except the skirt, the vent outlet, and the shield. You will also have to make an opening to add an electric heating element. If you go this route, make sure that it can be removed for repairs and not welded into place.

When I was in Scotland I went to a brewery with just such a kettle. It was very clean looking, and I could see going this way just for simplicity. They didn't even have a whirlpool, and only created cask ale, and darn fine ale at that. Because there was no direct flame they could decorate the Grundy with wood. It looked nice.

Electric Grundy Brew Kettle

By the way, if you are using a Grundy for a brew kettle, you will not be able to achieve 7 barrels of finished beer. While the Grundy is 7 barrels, you need enough headroom in your brew to avoid a boil over. In my first brewery, I generally could get 5.8 barrels of finished product, which I deemed adequate for our needs.

If you choose to use a dairy tank, your choices are many. These pictures illustrate some styles that would work well. For seven barrels you will want a kettle to hold 300 gallons, to allow enough head space and avoid a boil over.

Dairy Tank

You will be able to do the same modifications to these tanks as you would a Grundy, with one addition; they may also be jacketed, which would allow you to boil in the kettle by circulating steam through the jackets.

If they are jacketed and the jackets can hold pressure, you will need a boiler to produce the steam, which can be gas fired, or electric. You will need to involve your state boiler inspector in this process to make sure you comply with all the rules of your location. But when I talk about steam, I usually refer to low pressure, which is about 15 psi. These tanks have jackets on them already that were made for glycol and can hold about 15 psi. I have seen steam hooked directly to these jackets and they work great. By the way, steam is one of the most efficient methods for heating liquid in your kettle.

It has been difficult to find kettles as of late, especially for the students of our immersion course so I contacted Tom Bennett of Bennett Forgeworks, www.forgework.com, who I convinced to manufacture them right here in Ridgway. He is a master of his craft and they are better quality and cheaper than Chinese (I receive no compensation for recommending him). This is just another possibility.

Forgeworks Direct Fired 7 BBL Kettle

Heat Exchangers

You will need an effective way to cool the wort down to your desired temperature for yeast that is faster than the typical home brewer method. The general rule is to have the wort in the fermenter and on yeast within 45 minutes from the time the flame is off the kettle, if you want to avoid off-flavors developing. To do this you need a commercial heat exchanger.

Typical plate heat exchanger

If you buy a used one, you will want to take it apart to make sure all the plates are clean and the gaskets are in good condition. If they are not, they will need to be replaced before your first brew. When taking the exchanger apart, be very careful to keep the plates in the correct order, so that you can reassemble it to work.

Typically there is a water inlet and a separate wort inlet on one side, and the wort and water outlet on the other. Looking at the example above you see the outlets to the left. There is a temperature gauge inline to show you the temperature of the wort as it leaves the heat exchanger. You can adjust the temperature by controlling how quickly the wort flows through the plates. The faster the wort goes through the heat exchanger, the less contact time it has with the plates that are being chilled by water, hence the warmer the wort. Don't worry though; it is easy to dial in.

A good source for new heat exchangers is Hamby Dairy supply, www.hambydairysupply.com. With typical water temperatures of around 55 degrees, a heat exchanger with about 70 plates should work. You should talk to them first to make sure that there is sufficient surface area on the plates to cool boiling wort to 70 degrees, given your city water temperature.

Oxygen Systems

When the wort exits the heat exchanger you need a system to oxygenate your wort before it moves on to the fermenter. I put a valve on the outlet of the heat exchanger, connect an oxygen infuser to one side of the valve and a hose on the other side of that. As the wort passes through, it goes past what is called an oxygenating stone that diffuses pure O2 into the wort. By adjusting the valve you can speed up or slow down the flow, which will regulate the temperature of the wort.

There are commercial products available for this purpose, or you can simply make one using stainless tees.

Oxygenating Set Up

Oxygen Stone

The first picture is a ready-made O2 system. The ball valve is attached to an oxygenating stone inside the cylinder. Also there is a built in site glass to the right, which is great for checking wort clarity.

The next two pictures show two tees, (1 inch and 1.5 inch). The third picture shows a typical carbonating stone, which can be used for oxygenating. It is inserted into one end of the tee. The wort comes in through the opposite end and out the side. This works well. You could also buy a sight glass separately to place in line as well.

Fermentation Vessels

There are two extremely important pieces in the fermentation puzzle. The first is a sanitary surface. By this I mean there are no scratches or dings on the inside surface areas where infection could occur. So you need stainless steel that has what is called in the industry a “mirror finish”. This must include all welds. So when looking at tanks, you need to inspect the inside very carefully. Run your fingers along all the welds, and under any manways, etc. feeling for smooth surfaces.

Scratches can be polished out but you should leave that to a professional. The polishing uses a type of sandpaper and it is important that what is used was new and never used on regular steel as it would imbed that steel into the stainless, causing future corrosion. As I said use a professional if you find a good tank but it has some scratches you want to eliminate.

The second piece is the tank's ability to be temperature controlled. As you are aware, during the fermentation process, the wort temperature increases. If the temperature goes above the yeast's tolerance, you will develop off-flavors in your beer. So, the tank needs to be jacketed in a way that keeps the temperature from rising above 72 degrees. Once you reach 72 degrees, coolant must circulate through the jackets bringing the beer temperature back to a safe level.

Before I go on I would like to diverge a bit. When I first started thinking about doing my own brewery in 1992, I stumbled upon McMenamins in Portland, Oregon. These neighborhood brewpubs use the quintessential Frankenbrew systems. They do not all use temperature-controlled fermentation, (some do, some don't). In fact the beer often goes directly out of their fermenters (regular Grundy tanks) to their kegs. Their beer is cloudy, yeasty, slightly flawed, and wonderful. If you are seriously considering a Frankenbrew system, I recommend that you take an Oregon vacation and visit one of their small pubs. Check out www.mcmenamins.com.

So, what are your options? One of the easiest would be a dairy tank. It is perfectly sanitary, it is insulated, and it is jacketed. On the downside however, it is an open fermenter – albeit one with lids, it takes up more room than a cylindrical tank, and harvesting yeast is a bit more difficult. I have used these tanks and won gold, silver and bronze medals at the World Beer Cup, and Great American Beer Festival, so I know they make good beer.

Milk Chiller Dairy Tank

Another option would be a jacketed cylindrical tank. You can occasionally find Grundy's that have been jacketed. If you can't, there is a way you can jacket them yourself. I did it with my first brewery by taking lengths of soft copper and welding them to a header. Then I wrapped the jacket around the tank and used stainless straps to attach it tightly it to the tank. Next I used a rubber mallet and gently pounded the copper tubes to slightly flatten them along the surface of the tank. It was not beautiful, but it worked. It maintained the fermentation temperature, and at the end of fermentation I could lower the temperature to about 45 degrees, which was enough to make the yeast flocculate out and we were able to transfer clear beer.

Your next choice could be a white wine fermenter. I kept looking at these things and wondering why they couldn't be used for beer. I bought one just to find out and they work great. I get them from St. Pats of Texas, www.stpats.com. They cost $3,300 brand new. They are jacketed but not insulated, although I have found they do a terrific job of cooling. They are less than three feet in diameter, which means you can cram a lot of them into a tiny space, and as a bonus they look great.

Letina Z1000-C

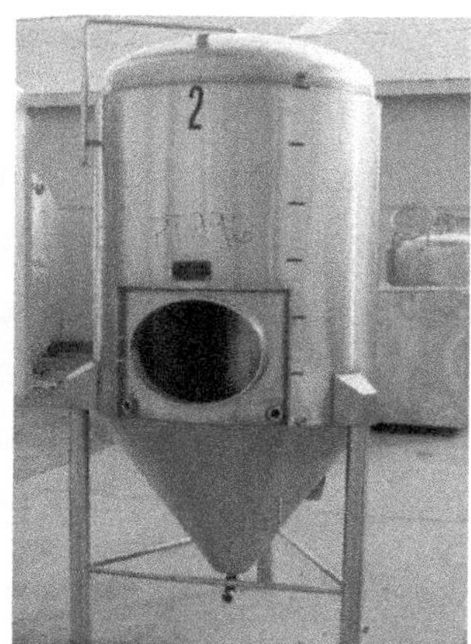

Uni-Tank

One of the best fermenter's you can find is the conical. This is an American invention, and the one you have probably seen in most breweries. It is called a Uni-Tank because it is several tanks in one. Due to its unique shape, it works as a fermenter, and at the end of the fermentation period, the yeast flocculates to the bottom of the cone where it can easily be harvested. Then the beer can remain in the same tank to condition. These are more expensive than the dairy tanks. A typical price would be $6,000 and up.

Conditioning Tank

Similar to the fermentation tank, the same characteristics are necessary in the conditioning tank, except it does not need to be jacketed. If you are using a cold room, which you will no doubt need to keep your kegs in, you can keep your conditioning tanks there as well.

For the correct conditioning tank you will need a tank that can hold pressure, as you will be carbonating the beer in this tank as well. This is why a dairy tank won't work for a conditioning tank as the simple lids do not seal or hold pressure. However if you plan to just carbonate in the kegs, then of course you could use this type of tank. I'll go over that in more detail in the carbonating section.

So because this tank is not jacketed, it is usually less expensive. For the longest time the cheapest tanks you could find were Grundies. They are hard to find used anymore and if you find one they cost about $1,800. Another alternative is Chinese.

Wenzhou Shuangding Machinery Co., Ltd has excellent 7 BBL serving tanks for about $2,000 plus shipping. Contact Annabel who is the General Manager at wzshuangding@hotmail.com for a current price sheet.

7 BBL Serving Tank From Annabel

Keg Cleaner

Even if all the beer you produce is for in-house use and all the beer goes right from your conditioning tanks to your taps, you will need some kegs in inventory for beer festivals, special customer orders, and to drain off the last beer from a tank so that you can fill it with fresh beer.

There are commercial keg cleaning systems available, and often you can find them used, but it is possible to build your own as well. A typical set up in a small brewery involves a stainless steel sink with stainless angle iron brackets on top to support an upside down keg. Below the sink you should have at least a half horsepower pump. The drain should have two outlets, one that goes to a floor drain, and one that can recirculate back to the pump inlet. The following illustration shows how this works.

Keg Cleaning Set Up

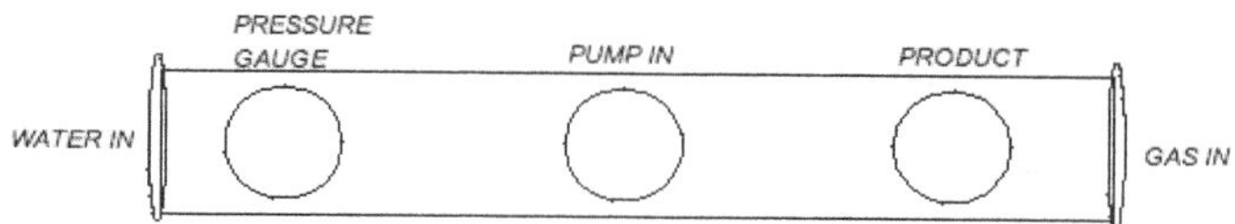

1. Attach pump outlet to middle TC
2. Attach keg filler to Product TC
3. Add hot Acid #6 to sink
4. Run keg filler drain hose to floor sink
5. Open keg filler gas outlet to drain keg
6. Open keg filler product inlet
7. Turn on hot water to rinse keg. Rinse twice
8. Replace keg filler outlet to drain back into sink
9. Turn pump on. Set valve on pump at 15psi and run for 2 minutes
10. Allow acid to drain back into sink. Push with burst of CO2
11. Run keg filler drain hose to floor sink
12. Turn on hot water to rinse keg.
13. While final rinse, turn CO2 on. When all water is rinsed from keg turn off drain hose valve and allow CO2 pressure to build to 10#.
14. Turn all filler valves off and remove keg.

Keg Filler/ Cleaner

American Sanke Valve

One of the most important pieces you will use in your brewery is your keg filler, which also is what you use to clean kegs. To build one start by taking a simple American Sanke valve and removing the check valves from the inlet (top) and the outlet (side). Foxx equipment (www.foxxequipment.com) sells a ball valve with beer nut thread that will screw onto the inlet and outlet of the Sanke. Attach a braided hose to the top inlet after the ball valve. Make it about five feet long, and at the other end put a 1.5 inch tri clamp to ¼ inch male hose barb. Attach a larger braided hose to the outlet side of ball valve of the Sanke.

Keg Filler

Pieces and Parts

A "T.C." or tri-clamp, is the type of fitting used in most small American breweries. Most likely you will be using a 1.5 inch "T.C." Brewing systems under 15 barrels really have no need for anything larger. You can recognize it as a "T.C." fitting by the recessed circular groove around the perimeter, as in this example of a sample valve with a "T.C." fitting.

Sample Valve

Here are some basic fittings you will want in your brew house.

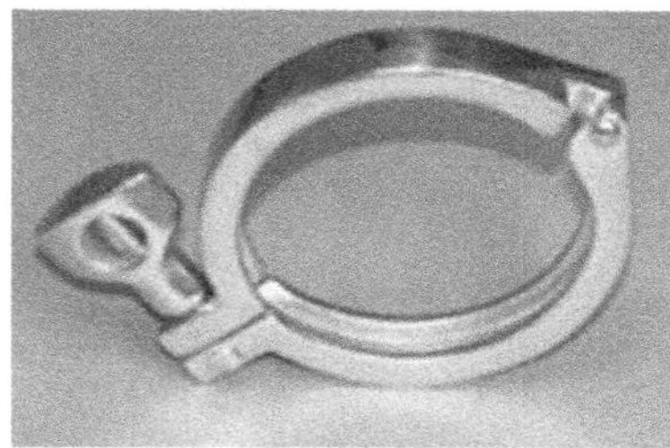

Clamp

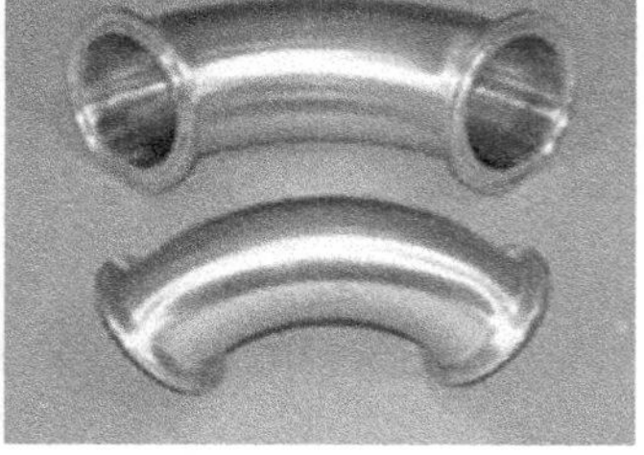

Elbows

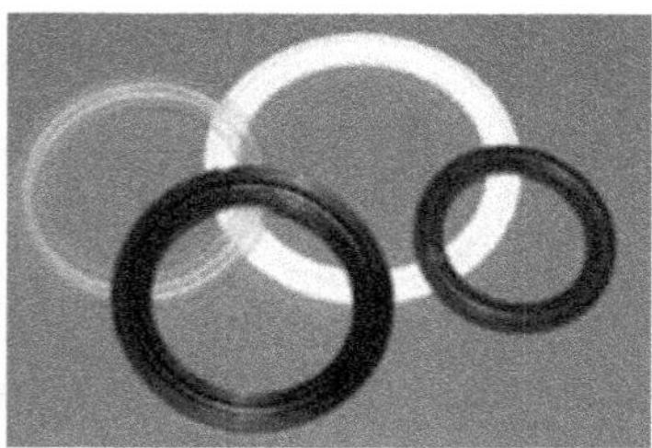

Gaskets

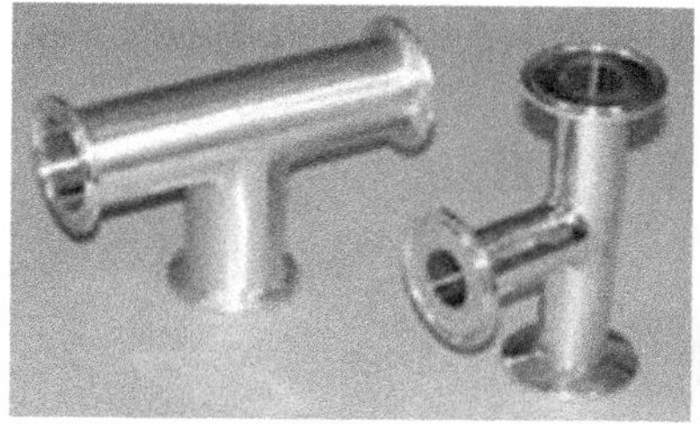

Tees

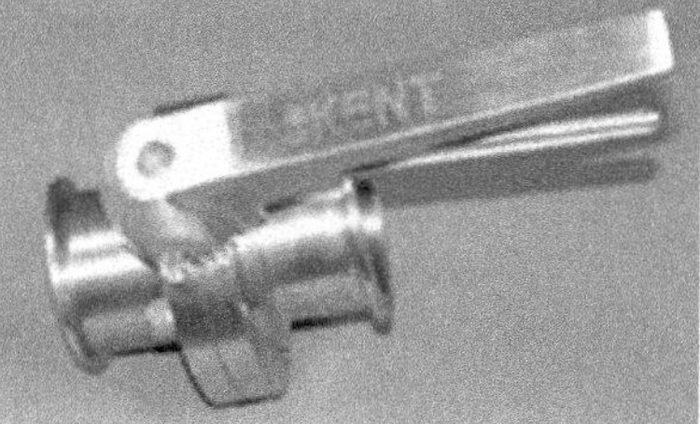

Butterfly Valve

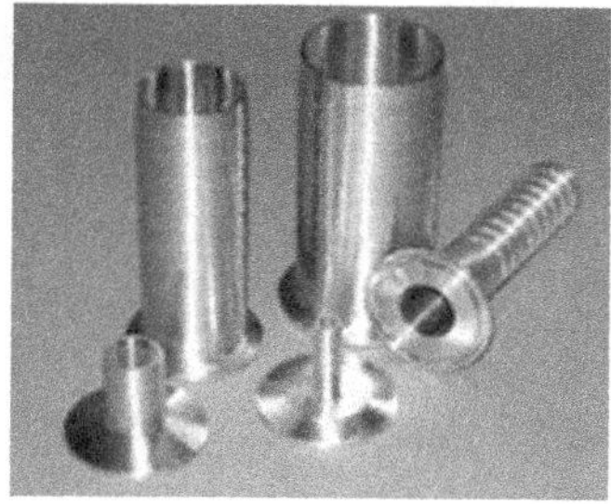

Hose Barb to TC Fittings

Brewery Hose

You don't want to go cheap with the hoses in your brewery. There are three types you will most likely have.

The first is a simple, but high quality garden hose. This is what you will use for general cleaning, spraying tanks out, spraying down the floor, etc. They are not expensive and easy to move around the brewery.

The most important one is for the hot side of the brewing process. They are super heavy duty, can take heat and pressure, and give no off-flavors to the product. You order them according to lengths. Your source may offer those with " TC" ends banded on. You will need at least two, depending on your brewery layout; one on the outlet of your kettle going to your pump, and one from the pump to the heat exchanger, or wherever in your brew process. The typical cost of this kind of hose is about $12 per foot.

Hot side hose with "TC"

The third one is able to handle product under pressure, though not extremely hot. It still needs to be of a quality that will not transfer any flavors to the product. I recommend clear vintners hose. I like clear because you can see the product move through, and the visual aid helps. If you cannot get this with the "TC" fittings, you can purchase appropriate "TC" to hose barb adaptors and band it yourself. This type of hose is easy to cut and deal with. It costs around $3 per foot.

Grant

This is an optional devise but one that I highly recommend. It is essentially a capturing vessel placed between the mash tun and the brew kettle. Rather than pumping from the mash tun to the kettle you gravity feed into this vessel.

The way it works is to take an elbow from the outlet of the mash tun and an extension that drops down into the grant so that the outlet is below the level of the wort in the grant. This prevents the wort from being aerated. The wort exits the grant through a hose to a pump. The wort moves from there to the bottom inlet of the brew kettle.

The trick is to match the flow from the mash tun to the grant with the pump to the kettle. I start with the pump off and slowly run off to the grant from the mash tun. When the level of the wort is close to the top of the grant, I start the pump so that just enough exits to halt the rise in the level of the wort. It takes a little fiddling to get it just right.

You can easily make a grant. Simply take a battered old keg and cut the top off. In the bottom of the grant on the side, add a 1.5-inch "TC" fitting.

Grant

Pumps

In brewing you need to use only sanitary pumps. These will be centrifugal pumps and made of stainless steel with 1.5-inch "TC" fittings on the inlet and outlet. For a small brewery a half-horsepower motor should be all you need. If you start using larger tanks, you should go to a 3/4 to 1 horsepower motor for better tank cleaning. I'll get to that later.

Pump

You can get by with one pump depending on your ability to have your equipment positioned is such a way that you can gravity from some tanks to others. If not, it is a good idea to have two. I like the insurance of having two, just in case one breaks down during a brew, you will have a backup. Sooner or later this WILL happen.

Testing Equipment

For a barebones brewery, you still need the ability to test your process to assure you are making great beer. Here is what I recommend for the simplest option:

- Good quality laboratory hydrometers, not home brew ones
- Good quality hand held pH meter with calibrating solutions
- Good quality gram scale

For something better, add:

- Imhoff Cone for testing solids in wort
- Microscope and hemocytometer for doing yeast cell counts
- Water test kits

For a truly good lab set-up, include:

- Zahn-Nagel CO2 tester
- Centrifuge
- Autoclave
- Gram Stain test kits

Now the truth is we won just as many competitions with our barebones testing equipment, but if you start to sell in package, you need to be super consistent and have the confidence that your product will have sufficient shelf life for the wholesale market. These are just suggestions. You can take it as far as you want to go.

Equipment Sources

If you have a bucket of money you can purchase a nice brewing system that is ready to go from one of the excellent manufacturers such as JV Northwest, or Specific Mechanical. However, if you are on a budget, and that is what this book is about, then you will want to piece your system together.

Now that you know what type of equipment you are looking for and all the options you have for tanks, here is a list of web-sites I cruise almost daily looking for what is available. Don't wait until you have your space built out before you start buying your equipment because you may not be able to find any. Have a place to store things and start buying today. It takes some time to put a system together this way.

My first daily stop is www.probrewer.com. This site has an excellent classified section and is easy to browse. There is also plenty of information sharing as well. Things go fast here, so know what you are looking for, how much you are willing to spend and contact the seller immediately with an offer.

I also check in on www.ebay.com. Do a search on process tanks, stainless steel tanks, or just something like, "200-gallon tank", for things that can be made into a kettle or a mash-tun. You can also search for sanitary pumps, kegs, tap towers, etc. Almost anything you need for your pub you can find here.

Along those same lines, you can do a search on www.craigslist.org. It is little harder to search, but you can find restaurant equipment in there that is local. It is also a good place to find restaurants for lease.

One of my favorite places to look for tanks is www.dairyengineering.com. They have a large list of used tanks. This is a good place to find dairy tanks that work great as fermenters, plus a wide range of tanks arranged by gallons. In fact, there are many other companies like Dairy Engineering and you can find them by doing a Google search for "used dairy equipment".

I recommend you also join the Association of Brewers organization. There are plenty of benefits, but one of them is the Brewers Resource Guide. This is a "Yellow Pages" of sources for everything you need in a brewery. It also lists facts about the industry and all the breweries in the US and Canada.

Glycol Chiller

One thing that separates the home brewer from the professional is having a temperature-controlled fermentation. This is accomplished by having chilled propylene glycol running through a loop through the jackets on the fermentation vessel. Then, when called upon by rising fermentation temperatures, glycol can be channeled through bringing the fermenting beer temperature back down to tolerable levels to protect the strain of yeast employed.

Most professional glycol chillers can be very expensive power hogs, but what I offer here is a simple Frankenbrew solution for the seven-barrel brewery. This is inexpensive and something you can plumb yourself.

I have found that a small glycol chiller used for beer lines is sufficient for two seven-barrel fermenters, possibly even three. These can be found from draft suppliers like Foxx Equipment, for about $1,500. The one I use has a ¾ HP compressor and a fifteen- gallon glycol reservoir. It comes with its own pump. The pump is normally used for pulling the glycol into a trunk line that would keep the beer lines cold.

To connect this to your system, place the glycol unit above the fermenters. Using one inch PVC, make a large loop to tee off a line to each fermenter. Then have another line coming from the fermenter back to that loop. What is important in this system is to put a simple valve in between where the glycol feeds the jacket on the fermenter and where it returns. You slightly close off this valve to create a restriction. Then, when the solenoid valve opens calling for glycol to the fermenter this becomes the path of least resistance so the glycol circulates through the jacket, rather than continuing on its loop.

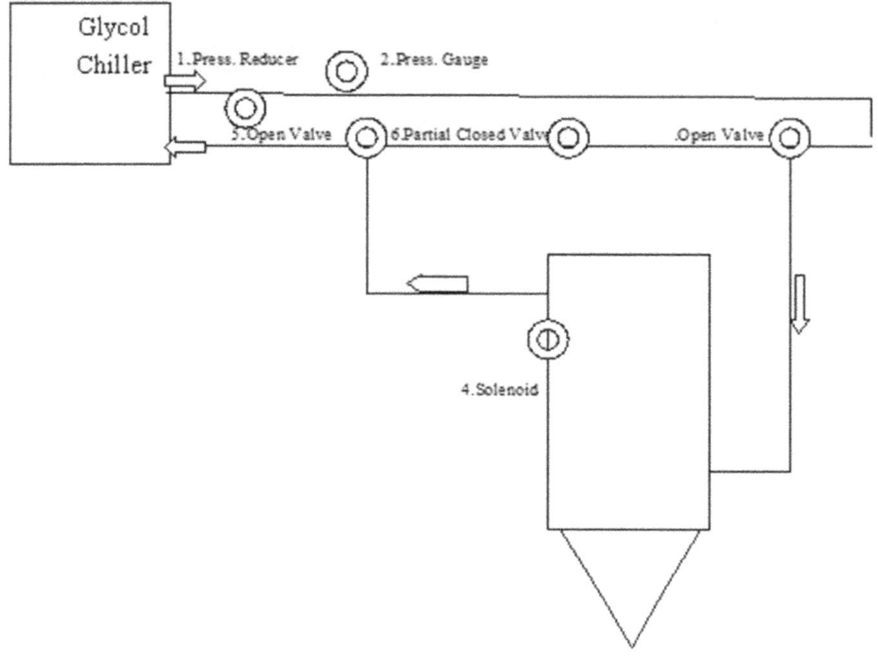

1. Pressure reducer set so line pressure is below 15psi
2. Pressure gauge to monitor line pressure
3. Valve to send glycol to fermenter. (Should be completely open.)
4. Solenoid valve on outlet of fermenter. It is on the higher one because the flow should be from bottom to top, allowing any bubbles to bleed off.
5. Valve for the return of glycol to the loop. Should completely open.
6. With the solenoid valve off to the fermenter, and glycol only going through the loop, close this valve slowly until the pressure valve reads about 14psi. When the solenoid valve is open then that is the path of least resistance and it forces the

glycol through the jacket. But when the solenoid is closed the pressure never gets above 15psi so it won't hurt your tank.

FOOD

You can skip this step if you are planning on only serving beer in your tasting room and not getting a food license. When we had our packaging brewery, we served popcorn so people had something to munch on with their pints. You do not need a food license for this. However if you would like to add a simple food menu the following section will help explain what is needed.

For explanation purposes I will assume you will offer a simple Panini menu. It is very inexpensive to add to your operation and the grilled sandwiches are excellent.

If you already have a restaurant, most of the following is probably already in place. If not, then here is a short guide on what you will need. You will need to contact your county health department for their specific guidelines. They will give you a booklet that details everything they require.

Kitchen Equipment

It is possible that, if you are taking over an existing restaurant, you will have a lot of the kitchen equipment in place. Even if you are offering a simple menu of Panini sandwiches, there are some basic equipment purchases you need to make.

Used vs. New

I think by now you can gather that I'm a big proponent of used equipment! However, there are some new things you should consider.

Topping that list is **refrigeration**. If you buy a used refrigerator, you have no idea how it may have been abused. The piece of equipment may have been located in a place that was hot, which kept the compressor working overtime. Perhaps the previous owner did not clean the compressor screens on a regular basis. Consider the age of the unit. A compressor has a life of about 5 years, and is the most expensive part of the refrigerator. Refrigerators usually come with a 5-year warranty. If you buy a new one, and you take care of it, that will be one thing you will not have to worry about for years. However if you buy used, you can rest assured that it will probably break down on a week end when you need it most and getting someone to come out and fix it will cost time and a half.

If you do decide to buy a used refrigerator, check the date on the unit. Ask if the compressor has been changed out. See if the compressor screens are clean and in good shape. Also check the gaskets around the doors to see that they are not coming apart and make a good seal. You may find an old unit almost for free, in which case you could go ahead and spend the $500 to replace the compressor and a little extra for gaskets etc., and basically have a new unit for half the price.

Basic kitchen necessities including sinks, pots and pans, inserts, dishes and utensils can be purchased used. They have no moving parts that can break. Anything that has a motor on it, such as a slicer, mixer, hood with ventilation, must be purchased with more care. Basically, check to see that the item is clean and the motor runs free without any strange sounds (bad bearings) coming from it. With these items, you can expect to pay anywhere from ten cents to fifty cents on the dollar compared to new.

To serve grilled sandwiches in your brewpub, you will need basic equipment. I like this route, as it is a very simple way to start. It is especially good if you have no restaurant experience. Here is a list of kitchen equipment you will need.

- Commercial panini maker
- Refrigerated sandwich prep table
- Freezer
- Stainless steel prep table
- Commercial slicer
- Three compartment sink
- Hand washing sink
- Assorted bowls, knives, spatulas, spoons

You can see the list is pretty simple. In addition to the kitchen equipment you will need baskets with wax paper to serve the sandwiches in and paper napkins. We served the panini sandwich with chips. No silverware is involved. The par number of sandwiches is made up every day. When a customer wants a panini with their beer, the bartender goes to the kitchen, unwraps a sandwich and pops it into the panini maker. They then set the timer for 4 minutes, set up the basket with chips and go back out to the bar. When the timer goes off, they pull out the sandwich, cut it in two, place it in the basket and serve it with a napkin.

There is no need for a kitchen-person as the bartender can prep the sandwiches before the shift. There is also no need for a dishwasher. The few spoons, knives or insert pans, can be easily washed up in the three-compartment sink at the end of the shift.

Granted this is barebones food service, but if you are unfamiliar with restaurants, this may be a good way to go. For sandwich ideas, just search on-line for "panini menus" and you will find all sorts of great sandwiches to make. Later we'll go into specifics about how to run your kitchen.

Chapter 8

EARLY PURCHASES

There are some things you need to order well in advance of your opening date. You can use this as a checklist of to-do items as you are building out your brewery space.

Logo

I assume by now you have a name for your brewery. With that name you will want a logo that can be plastered on stickers, hats and t-shirts. It will also go on any labels you come up with for packaging. This may be an area you are tempted to go cheap, but remember that the quality of this logo will sell your merchandise, beer, and even the location of your brewpub for years to come.

One thing I've learned the hard way is to keep your colors simple in the design. At Il Vicino, our wood oven pizza brewpub, our logo had only one color, and it was inexpensive to reproduce on hats, tee shirts, and growlers. Somehow though I lost my marbles when I did the Palisade Brewery. That logo was beautiful, but is was a four-color design, and every time I had to re-produce it, I got clobbered with high set up and print fees. So now with Colorado Boy I am somewhere in the middle. The logo has two colors and I have a one-color version as well.

I also recommend having a professional do it for you. At our current brewery I hired Jared Jacobs, who is an award winning logo designer. His web site is www.sundaylounge.com, and you can get an idea of what professional logos look like.

Sign

Check with your building and zoning department for their restrictions on signs. They will have it in writing what kind of sign and size is allowed at your location. You should also check with your landlord for certain restrictions for size and style of the sign. Most towns and cities require a sign permit. To acquire a sign permit you will have to present a drawing with measurements, and then pay a fee to have the sign put up.

Most sign companies need at least a month to make and install the sign. I would give them two months to be safe. This is why this is one of the first things you must do on this list.

Merchandise

Plan on selling at a minimum, hats and tee shirts in your pub. It can easily mean an extra two or three thousand per month in sales, as everyone likes a souvenir from a brewery. To have them on hand though from day one, give yourself some time to order them before you are open. Here is a list of things to consider.

Growlers come in clear glass and amber. There are also the regular shaped ones that you see everywhere and the fancy type with pewter handles. For my taste the basic clear ones are best. Yes I know it allows the beer to be light struck, but in my experience most folks just take them home and drink them before any damage is done to the beer. The clear ones are easy to fill because you can see the beer inside. Plus it is appealing to the customer when they can see all the pretty beer colors.

Types of Growlers

One mistake I often see is a one-color logo in black on the growler. This may look fine when the growler is empty, but remember that a lot of people will be buying growlers with dark beer inside and then the logo is obscured. So make the logo on your growler white or some other light color. For example the one on the left will look completely different filled with porter. Our growlers are one color – white.

Besides your logo, the company that prints your growlers will include a government warning required by law to be on all growlers. You also have space to add a paragraph or so about your brewery, or how to handle and store the growler, or possibly information about your brewing process or philosophies.

Once you have your growler label proof, you may have to submit the label to your state liquor board for approval. You will be informed of this when you apply for your brewpub license.

It will probably be six weeks from the time you first contact the company that makes the growlers until you receive your delivery. Keep that in mind when ordering. Give yourself plenty of time to have them on hand when you open.

Hats and **Tee Shirts** also need to be ordered at least one month before you open. If you want to start small, I recommend just one style of hat and one very cool tee shirt in an interesting color other than white. Keep in mind also that women like to buy hats and tee shirts even more than men, or so it seems in our experience. So offer smaller sizes, not just large and extra large.

Logo Glasses have been very popular at our pub. Because we are so small and it is easier to keep track of everything, I use logo glasses as our everyday glasses. At least with glasses you do not need different sizes and everybody wants them for home. If you have a larger place you may want plain glasses and just have the logo ones available for purchase. Logo glasses sometimes seem to walk out the door. Give yourself plenty of lead time when ordering these also.

Chapter 9

START BREWING

After about three or four months you will be contacted by the TTB (Taxation and Trade Bureau) regarding your application. Undoubtedly they will find small errors in your application. After some back and forth these will be corrected and they will schedule an appointment to come out for a site visit. For some reason they never did one for our current brewery, but came out for all the others. I have also heard from others, that the TTB does not come out to inspect all new breweries, but you should expect them just the same.

Make sure that your brewery looks in real life like the one you sent in with your application. That means placing the equipment in the same places you had it in your drawings. The one thing they will want to see more than anything is what is called the "Tax Determination Tank". This is your final tank where the beer is finished and ready for serving. It needs to be calibrated with marks on it so that you can tell how much beer it contains.

A Grundy tank has slash markings on the inside that you can see through the two sight glasses in the top. They mark up to five barrels British, which you can convert to American barrels. Or you can use a Tri Clamp fitting to ¼ inch hose barb and a clear tube. After you transfer your green beer from your fermenter to your conditioning tank, you can connect this to the bottom of the tank and hold it up along the side, open the bottom and beer will flow up the tube letting you see an accurate level. You will need to make markings on the outside of the tank for every ten gallons. You can use a small water meter to calibrate the tanks and make marks on the outside as you fill it with water. (Remember to sanitize the hose first, and make sure there is no pressure in the tank before you take a reading.) The TTB (Taxation & Trade Bureau) is most interested in getting their taxes. When other small questions or issues arise, you will find them very helpful and willing to work with you on site.

Once you have received your state license and Basic Permit from the TTB, you are finally ready to brew. In this section I will go through all the steps and methods we use to brew beer with a Frankenbrew system. We will also go through all the steps to get the beer to a glass.

Beer Recipes

A good place to start with your first recipe is a look at the style guidelines for what you plan to brew. Here is an example of a style guideline for American Pale Ale, from the Association of Brewers.

> "American Pale Ales range from golden to light copper-colored. The style is characterized by American-variety hops used to produce high hop bitterness, flavor and aroma. American Pales Ales have medium body and low to medium malty-ness. Low caramel character is allowable. Fruity-ester flavor and aroma moderate to strong. Diacetyl should be absent or at very low levels. Chill haze is allowable at cold temperatures."

Original Gravity (°Plato): 1.044-1.056(11-14°Plato)
Final Gravity (°Plato): 1.008-1.016 (2 – 4 °Plato)
Alcohol by weight (volume): 3.5-4.3% (4.5 – 5.5%)
Bitterness (IBU): 20 – 40
Color SRM (EBC): 4 – 11 (10 – 25 EBC)

The first paragraph describes what the pale ale should be like in general terms. From this explanation the brewer will decide what types of malts to use to give the beer its color, and malt character. In addition, the paragraph tells the brewer to use American hops, and how the hops are to be added. Since the description says the beer should have high hop bitterness, flavor and aroma, the brewer knows that a large amount of hops should be added at the beginning of the boil (bitterness), the end of the boil (flavor) and added to the conditioning when the beer is finished (aroma). In the description it also suggests "fruity-ester flavor and aroma" so the brewer will try to ferment a little more rapidly with a style of yeast that is known for contributing esters, which contribute a fruit-like character to the beer. To control diacetyl, the brewer will make sure to add a diacetyl rest at the end of the fermentation, thereby eliminating diacetyl, which is a butter flavor in the finished beer.

The second set of information gives the brewer targets to aim for in the recipe formulation.

"Original gravity" is the amount of sugar in the wort. This is accomplished by how much grain is added to a specific amount of water. The greater the amount of grain, the more concentrated the sugar will be. In the wine industry this measure of sugar is in Brix. In foods such as jelly, it is referred to as balling. In beer this is measured in degrees Plato.

Final gravity is the target that the beer will ferment out to. So the difference in the beginning Plato minus the end Plato will refer to the amount of sugar that has fermented out and gives us the alcohol by weight percentage.

Bitterness is measured in bittering units or IBU's (International Bittering Unit). The number of bittering units is dependent on the alpha acid content of the particular hops being used. A formula is used to tell the brewer how many pounds of hops to use at a particular alpha acid level to yield the desired IBU's.

Once you have determined what kind of beer you want to make, use a program like Pro Mash and plug in the desired bittering units and alpha acids and that will give you your basic recipe sized for the amount of barrels you are going to produce. All are for seven barrels. If you convert a Grundy to a brew kettle, you may need to change your batch size to six barrels.

INGREDIENTS

Malted Barley

Your base ingredient in making beer of course is malted barley. There are many different companies who sell it, and you can buy domestic, or from anywhere in the world, depending on what your preferences are for the beer you are trying to make. Malted barley comes in fifty-pound sacks in the US and Canada and 25 Kilo or 55 pounds elsewhere. Barley can also be purchased in large sacks of five hundred pounds, or delivered loose in bulk to your own grain silo in any amount.

Malted barley is sold in whole kernel. Some malting companies offer malts pre-ground. The larger the volume, as you would guess, the less you pay per pound. Also where the malt comes from dictates price as well. If the barley is grown and malted in North America, it is cheaper than European malt by as much as 25 cents per pound. And speaking of cost per pound, you can expect to pay from 27 to 70 cents per pound depending on what type of grain you are purchasing.

The base grain is called two-row or six-row malt. The two-row are more uniform in size and more typical in craft brewing. The numbers refer to the number of fertile flowers present but that is not important to you. These malts are very light in color and make up approximately 75% or more of your malt usage. If you order malt in bulk for a grain silo, it will be these types of malts you will be ordering.

The rest of the malts you can order are referred to as specialty malts. They are heated in a kiln to bring out color and other flavors in the malt. By using different combinations of malts in your beer recipe, you will develop your own unique flavors and beer color. Your malt supplier will send you samples of the types of malts they offer and suggested usages.

For a Frankenbrew set up, I suggest buying your malt pre-ground, at least at the beginning until you have a better handle on your brewing skills. You can always add a mill later, but for now it is one thing you don't have to think about.

Hops

As I said earlier, beer without hops is like food without salt, or better yet, a flower without an aroma. With hops, the fresher the better, which is almost impossible, because hops are only harvested once a year. Like wine grapes, hops grow on a vine. And like grapes, they come in different varieties, with different flavors and characteristics.

When the hops are picked they are evaluated according to alpha and beta acids, their oils, and their polyphenols. The important thing to look at however is the alpha acid content, as this will determine your recipe formulation in regard to bitterness. Each crop will come with all the significant numbers attached so you can make up your mind as to which hop varietals you want in your beer recipe.

Hops are picked fresh, dried and packaged in different ways. Whole hops are sold in large bales. There are some advantages to whole hops, but most small breweries do not use them as they take up a lot of space, and once you break into a bale, the hops will go stale in a short time if not used right away.

The majority of brewers use pelletized hops. While they may look like rabbit food, there are many advantages to using pellets. Basically in the pelletizing process, all the lupulin glands of the hops have burst open, thereby making them available in the brew faster and giving off a great nose for dry hopping. Plus they do not tend to get clogged in valves and heat exchangers, the way whole hops do. Also, they take up little room to store, as they can be packaged in small vacuum packed containers that will keep them relatively fresh until used.

Yeast

In theory, and in practice for some breweries, yeast only needs to be purchased once. If it is managed well, it can be regenerated forever. However, most breweries will buy yeast and use it for a specific amount of time, then purchase new yeast. Also a brewery will buy specialty yeasts for beers that are brewed only occasionally.

Fortunately there are good companies that supply different styles of yeast for you to purchase. Most suppliers have a free brochure that explains all the yeast varieties they offer and describe the characteristics of each yeast strain as well. They will also provide you with a lot of other valuable information to help you manage your yeast.

These companies prepare the yeast for you, then ship it to you overnight, packed cold and ready for you to use immediately. If you know you will need new yeast, you plan your brewing schedule around the arrival time of the yeast so that you can brew with it as needed. The suppliers will help you with the timing. Check out these web sites of suppliers, as they are chucky-chuck full of information.

TIP! If you order your laboratory testing supplies and culture media from the yeast suppliers, you'll find that they will give you a lot of free information to help you with your lab work as well.

Cleaning and Sanitizing Supplies

The chemicals you use to clean and sanitize your equipment are expensive and can be dangerous to handle, which is why it is important to understand how to use them correctly. For example I have seen many brewers use the glug rule when making up chemicals for cleaning. In other words, they hold the container upside down and count how many glugs before they stop pouring.

When using chemicals you should always use a measuring cup, as you will find it doesn't take that much chemical to do the job. Do not forget to always wear protective clothing and eye protection when performing any cleaning or sanitizing.

The basic chemicals I use for brewing are PBW for tank cleaning, Star San for sanitizing, Acid #5 for tank pacification, and Acid #6 for keg cleaning. I will go over their uses in more detail later.

Following is a "paper brew" to go through the steps of your brew day. We'll brew a 6-barrel batch of Pale Ale, on a converted Grundy system. We will use the following recipe, and I will go through the entire procedure from brew preparations, to tapping the final product.

Grain Pounds

2 Row Malt 270

Munich 10 L 31

Caramel 40 L 13
Total Malt Bill 314

Hops oz.
Cascade 1st addition 28
Simcoe 2nd addition 10
First Goldings whirl pool addition 22
Cascade dry hop addition 16
Simcoe dry hop addition 16
Total Hops 92

YeastChico (1056)

Brew Prep

The day before brew day, we will fill the brew kettle and heat the water to almost boiling. While the water is heating, we will weigh out the grain and put the grain bags in the brew house, to make sure they are at room temperature. Since we do not have a mill, we are using pre-ground malts.

Hoses can be set hooked up to the pump, so that in the morning once the kettle temperature is correct, we will be ready to pump our strike water over to the mash tun. We also set out our brewers log on the clipboard, our dust mask next to the paddle, and our favorite music queued up so the tunes are ready to go on brew day. Once the brewing water is about 200 degrees Fahrenheit, we turn off the kettle and make sure all the lids are on, so that the kettle loses as little heat during the night as possible.

Brew Day

Walk into the brew house and immediately check the temperature of the brew water and turn on the kettle. It will probably have lost about 20 degrees overnight, and will take about 30 minutes to get back up to the temperature you need to mash in.

We are shooting for a mash temperature of 153 degrees so experience tells us we are going to heat the brew water to 172. We know that we will lose about 20 degrees give or take in the transfer and mash in process.

Make up a bucket of sanitizing solution (I use iodine. Just enough to color the cold water) and fill it with gaskets, clamps, elbows, tees, and anything you will be using during the brew day. Also fill a spray bottle with fresh sanitizing solution to use around the brew house.

Based on previous brews, I know that to get the desired pH, I will add 4 ounces of phosphoric acid to the brewing water. To do this I lift the lid on the kettle and pour in the measured amount. Then I pump out of the bottom and back in through the whirlpool to mix the acid in.

Once the brewing water hits 172 degrees Fahrenheit, turn off the kettle and start pumping the water into the inlet of the mash tun. Our calculations say we need to mash in with 100 gallons of water, and since we are using a Grundy brew kettle, we can use the marks on the inside of the kettle, marked in British barrels, to tell us when we have transferred that much water.

As soon as the water has been transferred, we heat the remaining water in the kettle to use for sparge water. This we will heat to about 182 degree Fahrenheit, so that when it is transferred to the hot liquor tank and then from there to the mash tun it will be 170 degrees.

With the appropriate amount of water in the mash tun, we now start to add the malt. Starting with half the 2-row, using a paddle in between bags to even it out and break up any dough balls. In the middle of the mash in, add all the specialty malts, then the last of the 2-row. Go through the mash so that it is uniform with no dough balls, but do not over work it. Take the temperature of the mash and check the pH. Your target for the pH is about 5.2. If the mash is too high I add a small amount of phosphoric acid diluted with hot water stirred directly into the mash and re-test. If I need to raise it I use about 40 grams of calcium carbonate dissolved in hot water and stirred in. Note these numbers down on your log sheet. Close the lids to the mash tun for a 1-hour mash (our current mash tun has no lid and keeps the heat well).

Adding Pre-Milled Malt to Strike Water

Hydrometers, pH Meter, Gram Scale

Once the sparge water has hit the correct temperature, transfer that water to your hot liquor tank. Next take this opportunity to run a sanitation loop through your heat exchanger and the fermenter that you will be using that day. You will add the sanitizer to the fermenter. From the fermenter it goes to the pump, into the heat exchanger, through the

O2 infuser, then back into the fermenter through the top spray ball. This loop should run for about 30 minutes.

If you are not using a separate hot liquor tank because you either don't have the room or don't want to spend the money for an extra tank you will pump to the fermenter you are going to be brewing into. After sparging you can cool and re-sanitize the fermenter.

Once this step is completed, disconnect the pump set up (inlet and outlet hoses). Leave the one of the heat exchanger connected to the O2 infuser and hose. Disconnect the other end of the hose from the top of the fermenter, and connect it to the bottom inlet of the fermenter with a tee in between the hose and the inlet. Add a valve to the side of the tee. Make sure you spray sanitizer on anything you attach.

Next set your pump up for vorlauf, or a recirculation of the wort. To do this you will place your grant under the mash tun outlet. On the outlet add a 90-degree elbow with a straight piece after that, into the grant. Run a hose from the grant outlet to your pump. From your pump run a hose up to the side of the mash tun with two elbows that can hook on the side of the mash tun.

To vorlauf, start by slowly letting wort out into the grant. Once the wort level gets above the down tube, you can turn on your pump and slowly open the valve on the outlet of the pump to start pumping the wort back into the mash tun. Now the trick is to make sure that the wort coming into the grant is the same speed as the wort being pumped out. It should be slow enough to not cause any agitation in the wort. The wort going back into the mash tun should sluice along the side smoothly without picking up too much air. Be very observant, as soon as you turn your back on this set up, your grant will either over flow or go dry.

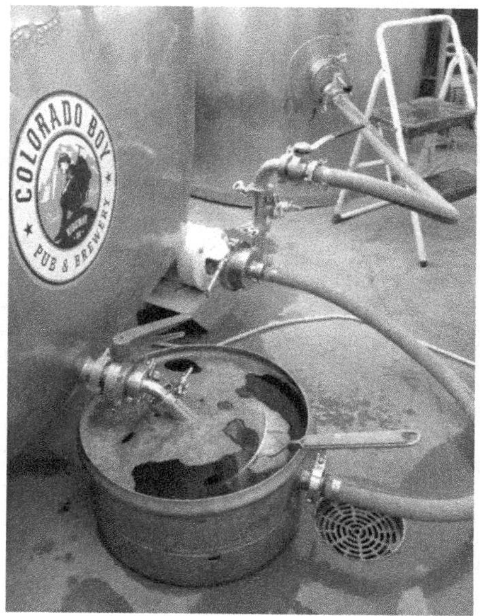

Grant

The object of this is to keep going until the wort that comes out of the mash tun is clear. This indicates that a good mash bed has set up, which means the mash is uniform and even with no gaps on the sides of the mash tun where water can run down instead of through the mash grain. To test this you can use an Imhoff Cone and take a 1-liter sample. Your sample should show less than 5ml of sediment in it. Of course, you can simply use a glass and take samples until it looks clear. Keep up the vorlauf until the wort is as you wish.

Once you achieve a good vorlauf, take the outlet hose from the vorlauf and attach it to the inlet on your brew kettle. Next, run a hose from your hot liquor tank to your sparge showerhead on your mash tun. Turn the sparge water on a slow setting and check the temperature, and enter it into the log. Your target should be no hotter than 170°F.

Sparging

Start the pump again and as slowly as possible, start transferring wort into the kettle. I say slowly because you want to extract as much sugar from the grain as possible. Keep an eye on your sparge water.

You want to keep about an inch of liquid above the grain bed. This process should take anywhere from 45 minutes to an hour and a half. I prefer a one-hour transfer.

Once the sparge runs out, just keep transferring wort until you reach your full kettle volume. Just before you stop the transfer, do a gravity reading of the last running. It should be no lower than 1.5° Plato.

As the wort fills the kettle, do not turn the kettle on until you have a sufficient amount of wort in the kettle. You want to avoid scorching or burning the liquid. On the other hand, don't wait until the kettle is full to turn it on. For this size batch about 25 gallons is enough, or when the wort reaches the bottom weld marks of a Grundy. You will find that by the time the kettle is full, it is already close to boiling.

Since you have some time before boil, and a half hour before the first hop addition, there is time to clean out the mash tun.

The simplest way is to let whatever liquid still in the mash drain away. Place a strainer in between the outlet and the grant to catch all the last of the grain so that it doesn't go into the drain. Then begin the work of shoveling out the spent grain. Spray all the inside clean. To hand wash the inside of the tank, use a light PBW solution and a green scrub pad and then rinse thoroughly. When you are finished your mash tun should be set up to recapture the hot water coming out of your heat exchanger during transfer. You can use this hot water for another brew or for cleaning at the end of the day.

Once you achieve a boil, the hot break, which is mostly protein, forms on the surface of the boiling wort. Use your strainer and remove this foam. You can get up to 70% of your proteins out of the wort this way. Make sure you write in your log sheet the exact time of your boil. I use a kitchen timer to start a countdown. I set this timer to 30 minutes.

At 30 minutes into your boil, add your first addition of hops. Add them slowly, because the pellets contain air, which can cause a boil over. If your kettle is really full, you may want to have a hose at the ready to spray some water on the surface to avoid over flow. Once you have your first hops in the kettle, the chance of a boil over is lessened for the next hop additions. In this recipe it calls for a second hop addition at 45 minutes after the beginning of the boil, so I re-set the timer to 15 minutes. With each step, set the timer to let you know when the next step will be.

Continue to monitor the boil for one and a half hours. During this time you can set up for your whirlpool. Do this by having a hose from the bottom outlet of the kettle to the pump, and then the other hose from the pump to the whirlpool inlet on the side of the kettle.

At 15 minutes before the end of the boil add kettle finings. This will help coagulate the trub and keep it in a nice pile at the bottom of the kettle after the whirlpool.

At the end of the boil, turn the kettle off and very slowly open the bottom outlet and the whirlpool inlet. There will be air in the hose, which could bubble up through the wort causing some of the wort to splash out of the kettle, so stand back. Turn the pump on and slowly open the butterfly valve on the pump to let the wort start flowing. I have noticed that if you open the pump all the way at the first, the pump will experience cavitation. Pump cavitation occurs when air bubbles get into the impeller of the pump creating a non-uniform pumping of liquid. By letting the pump heat up slowly you can alleviate this problem. After about a minute or two, you can then open the valve fully.

Whirlpool for 10 minutes, then turn the pump off and let it rest for 10 minutes. This will let the hops and trub that was whirl pooled to the middle settle to the bottom.

While the whirlpool is resting, go ahead and move the hose from the bottom outlet to the outlet above it (if you are using a Grundy). If the tank has a bottom outlet just on the side rather than the drawing from the bottom middle, you don't need to move this hose. Take the hose off the whirlpool inlet and hook it up to the heat exchanger inlet. Be careful, as the hose is full of boiling hot wort, so wear good gloves.

If you are pitching yeast using a ladle, go ahead and add the yeast to the fermenter at this point. If you are injecting it inline, set that up. If the yeast has been kept in a cooler I usually add it to the fermenter earlier in the brew so it has a chance to warm up.

Assuming the smallness of your operations you probably are not doing yeast cell counts. For ales just add 1½ pints of yeast per barrel of wort. That works great for me.

There should be a hose leading away from the bottom of the fermenter to the drain, so that the first running through the hose consisting of left over sanitizer goes to the drain and not the yeast in the fermenter. We call this our Transfer Tee.

To do this we use a tee with a valve on the side. We keep that valve open leading to the drain and the valve on the bottom of the fermenter closed until all the sanitizer has flowed out of the lines and we see just wort coming through, then we close off the drain valve and open up the fermenter valve.

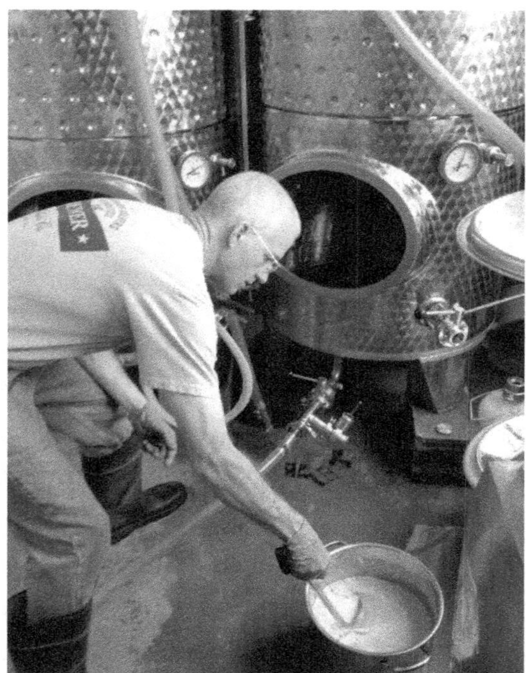

Brewer Elliott Bell Pitching Yeast

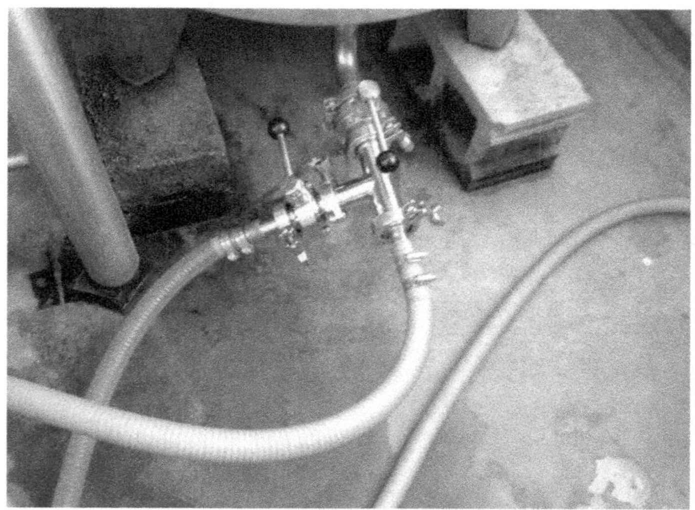

Transfer Tee

Turn the water on to your heat exchanger to get it cold. Then open the outlet on the brew kettle, and turn the pump on with the butterfly valve on the pump open just a bit, or enough to just let some wort through. It is better if the first wort into your fermenter is too cold rather than too hot. Once it is flowing you can adjust the temperature by opening the valve on the pump to let the wort flow faster. There should be a sufficient amount of sanitizer in the heat exchanger to give you time as it flows out your transfer tee to allow you to adjust the temperature. The temperature gage is on the oxygenating set up.

Once you have dialed the transfer in at 70°F, turn on the O2, so that the wort is getting a sufficient amount of oxygen. The transfer should take 45 minutes or less. Much of this will depend on temperature of the cold water running through your heat exchanger. If you are in a hot climate, you can cool the water down by filling one of your extra tanks in your cooler with water and using that. The 35 degree water from your cooler will allow a really fast transfer. Most city water is a constant 55 degrees.

I like to attach a hose from the water outlet of the heat exchanger to the clean mash tun to recapture this water. It should be around 120 to 140 degrees. You can use this free hot water for your rinse and cleaning water at the end of the day.

Continue to monitor the temperature of the wort going into your fermenter. As you get close to the end of the transfer, watch the bottom of your kettle to make sure that you are not sucking any of the hops or trub into the heat exchanger. You will know when to stop by just watching.

As soon as you turn off the transfer process, hook water up to the hose going from your kettle outlet to the heat exchanger and push the last of the wort through the hoses and heat exchanger to your fermenter. You will know when to turn the water off by looking at the site glass next to the oxygenating stone. As soon as you see the wort getting diluted, turn the water off.

Another option is to push the last of the wort through with CO2. This will avoid getting tap water into your wort.

Next, open the valve on the tee at the inlet to the fermenter that leads to the drain and continue pushing water through the system and into the drain until the water runs clear.

Finally, make sure you have a sanitized hose running from the top of your fermenter to a bucket of water, which will act as an airlock for the CO2 that will be bleeding off during the fermentation process.

Write down all the information on your log sheet, including temperature of transfer, time of transfer and amount of yeast pitched and what generation of yeast it is.

Clean Up

Attach a hose from the bottom of your kettle to a drain and open the outlet valve. Spray inside the kettle until free of all hops and trub. If you are using whole hops, you will need to catch these before they go into the drain. Pellets, which we are using for this recipe, can just be disposed of in the drain.

Next, prepare a cleaning solution. I prefer PBW, as it is safer and will not eat your skin. Mix this up in the brew kettle and heat it to the right temperature. If you are using the recaptured transfer water from your mash tun then it should already be hot enough.

Hook up all your hoses and fittings, to the pump, heat exchanger and brew kettle. Pump the cleaning solution out of the brew kettle in the **reverse direction** of the wort transfer. The return needs to go back in the brew kettle, which should have a spray ball in the top dome. This creates a loop. Run this for 30 minutes.

At the end of the cleaning cycle you want to pack the heat exchanger. This is the best method for cleaning it. To do this you have a valve at the product inlet of the heat exchanger and the product outlet. While the loop is going on, close the outlet, count to 2, then close the inlet and turn the pump off. Now your heat exchanger is packed under pressure with hot PBW. Take it out of the loop and leave it this way until your next brew, where you will rinse and sanitize it again.

Once everything has been cleaned, follow the same direction with fresh water, however this time you don't loop it, but rather let the finish water go down the drain. Do this for about 5 minutes, or until you are sure you have completely rinsed out the entire cleaning agent.

Finally, clean the floors and put everything neatly away. Polish the tanks and clean all the grain dust off. This is an important step as your customers are always watching the brew house and you want to leave a good impression.

Fermentation

For the next five plus days you will monitor your fermentation. Take a sample each day, and check the gravity. Write these readings on your brew log sheet. If you are consistent about checking at the same time each day, you can establish a fermentation pattern. You can graph this out and see a consistent pattern. When the pattern starts to change, as in slower fermentation, you will know that something has changed with your yeast.

Once the fermentation has stopped, let it rest for one more day. This is your diacetyl rest. After the rest, turn the temperature down on the fermenter to just above 32°F. This will cause the rest of the yeast to drop out of suspension. This should take about a day. Then the beer is ready to be transferred to your conditioning tank.

Conditioning

First you need to sanitize your conditioning tank. You do this the same way you sanitized your fermenter.

After you have cleaned your conditioning tank and rinsed it thoroughly, add the sanitizer into the tank and hook up your hoses to your pump. Include a tee with a valve at the bottom of the conditioning tank, just as we did on the fermenter before transfer. Again, we will pump out of the bottom of the conditioning tank then back into the top through the spray-ball. This will create a loop. Do this for 30 minutes, drain out the sanitizer and leave the tank empty.

Since this recipe calls for dry hopping, we will need to sanitize a hop bag. I use 5-gallon poly paint straining bags. I soak them in sanitizer, with a length of string that you use to tie off the bag.

Weigh out your hops and carefully put them into the sanitized hop bag, then tie this bag to your racking arm inside the conditioning tank. Wear gloves that have been sanitized. Spray more sanitizer around the man-way and close the tank up tightly.

If you are going to use finings, you will add this to the bottom of the tank at this time as well. The finings will mix with the beer as it transfers over. These days I am using Biofine Clear at about 1 ounce per barrel.

Open up the CO2 to the top of the tank and let it flow into the tank for about a minute. Release the pressure that has built up and leave the top open. The CO2 is heavier than air and will blanket the bottom of the tank as the beer flows in. It is very important that you leave the top valve open to let air escape as you transfer the beer. It's all physics.

Attach the inlet to the pump to the racking arm of the fermenter. Make sure that you spray the fermenters' racking arm with sanitizing solution before you attach the hose. There will still be a residual amount of sanitizer in the hose and pump from the loop you just did on the serving tank you are transferring into. Next move the outlet side of the hose on the pump to the bottom of the conditioning tank. There will still be a tee on the bottom of the tank. Open that valve up so that the initial fluid will not go into the conditioning tank, but rather to the drain. Monitor it until you see the beer at the tee, then close the drain valve and open up the tank inlet valve.

Without turning the pump you can now let the beer gravity feed to the conditioning tank. Remember you also need to open the top of the fermenter to avoid creating a vacuum as you transfer the beer out of the tank. Just by using gravity the two tanks will equalize. This is a better way to transfer the beer. Once the beer has stopped flowing you need to turn the pump on to transfer the rest.

To clean the fermenter, just repeat the same process you used with the brew kettle. You only clean and rinse it. Always wait until just before you need it to sanitize.

Yeast Harvesting

Since we are not talking about using conical fermenters, you will be harvesting right out of the bottom of the fermenter.

Once the beer has finished transferring, open up the door to the fermenter. If the racking arm was properly placed there should be very little beer sitting on top of the yeast. I sanitize a stainless steel ladle and first skim off any remaining beer and dump it into the drain. Then I start scooping out the yeast and putting it into a sanitized stainless stockpot, or a keg yeast brink if you have one. I take the yeast from the middle of the slurry rather than the sides or the very bottom. There is a good description of yeast harvesting methods in the free lab book online at www.brewingscience.com.

I gather enough yeast to fill the container about 2/3 full, leaving enough space for the yeast to expand during cold storage. I use yeast for about 10 generations before replacing with new yeast.

Carbonation

After one to two weeks of conditioning, the beer is ready to carbonate and tap. The amount of time it takes to carbonate depends on whether you have your carbonating stone in the side of your conditioning tank, or the bottom. Also of course it depends on the pressure and temperature of the CO2 in the vessel and beer. As you are using a Grundy that can only hold 15 PSI, let's look at your carbonation stone placement.

The best way is to have a 1.5 inch TC opening about a third of the way up the wall of the tank. Here, you insert a clean and sanitized stainless steel carbonating stone before you add your beer to be conditioned.

When you are ready to carbonate, allow the CO2 to flow though the stone slowly. Set your regulator at 12 psi. When the pressure gauge gets up to 12 psi, you are at equalized pressure. Using the pressure relief valve at the top of the tank, burp off half the pressure and let it build up again. Do this about five times during the course of the day. The way to test your carbonation level is to tap the tank and try the beer. I'll get to another way to test in a bit.

If you don't have a TC opening in the side of your tank, you can attach a carbonating stone to a straight pipe, then attach that to the bottom port of your tank. Once it is attached, open the bottom of the tank and turn on the CO2. The gas will bubble up from the bottom and carbonate the beer. This method takes a bit longer however because there is less surface contact with the beer. On the plus side, you can get away with just one carbonating stone because it doesn't need to stay in the tank. This method is the more difficult of the two.

There is a third method for carbonating your beer. Simply rack off the beer into your kegs. Pressure the kegs up to about 30 psi. With pressure on the keg, tilt it on its base and rock it back and forth one hundred times. Do that about six times total during the course of the day. To test you need to drop the pressure back down to about 12 psi then tap the keg and test it. Only do this if this is the only way you can afford to get started in this business. Carbonating all your beer this ways hardly makes life worth living.

To properly test CO2 levels in beer there is nothing that beats a Zahm-Nagel CO2 tester. These are pricey, but you can occasionally find them used on Ebay or www.probrewer.com. Typical costs for used ones run from $800 to $1,000. If you go to their web site www.zahmnagel.com, you will get the best description of how they work. I love these things, because by using one you will hit a perfect carbonation level every time. Your customers will appreciate the consistency and if you are going to package your product it is a necessity.

Zahm-Nagel CO2 Tester

Getting It To The Tap

Let's start with the simplest method. When you build your brewery, position the cold room directly behind the bar so that the back of the bar shares the same wall as the cooler. You can then run the taps directly through the wall into the back of the bar in a horizontal alignment.

To make the taps most effective and efficient, make a cutout on the inside of the cooler so that the tap shanks are exposed to the cold air. This will allow the beer to stay as cold as possible because it will actually transfer the cold air onto the metal of the tap itself. This helps the beer maintain a consistent temperature.

If your cold room is not close to the taps, you can use a glycol chilled beer line called a trunk line. This is a separate small glycol chiller attached to a hose whereby chilled glycol is pumped out the hose then back through a return. Regular beer lines surround this glycol line, and the whole thing is wrapped in black foam insulating material.

You can purchase this hose in any length. In our brewpub in Salida, Colorado we had a 50-foot run to the taps and had no problem with consistent beer delivery – a word of caution however; do not run root beer through this line. The root beer flavor is so strong that it will actually go through its beer line and into the other lines in the hose, resulting in all your beers tasting like root beer.

The third way to get the beer to your taps is simply to use a refrigerated keg cooler at the bar and keg everything. I did this at the Palisade Brewery, but it is a hassle if you are the least bit busy as you are constantly wheeling out kegs and replacing them when empty.

I like the first method best as you can run the beer directly off of your conditioning/serving tank. This way there are no kegs to change out, and less kegs to clean and maintain. If you include a window in the back bar that looks into the cooler, it's a great reminder to your customers that your beer is fresh.

From the bottom of your serving vessel you use a tri-clamp to a hose barb to deliver your beer to the taps.

1.5 Inch Tri-Clamp to ¼ Inch Hose Barb

To push your beer to the tap you can either use CO2 or Beer gas, which is usually a mix of 75% Nitrogen and 25% CO2. I run the hose into the cooler from the tank and regulator but then feed individual regulators dedicated to each serving vessel. That way if there is a gas leak somewhere I can isolate the problem by turning off all gas and checking each tank at a time. I can also play with different pressures depending on whether I am doing a beer to a Guinness style nitro tap or regular tap.

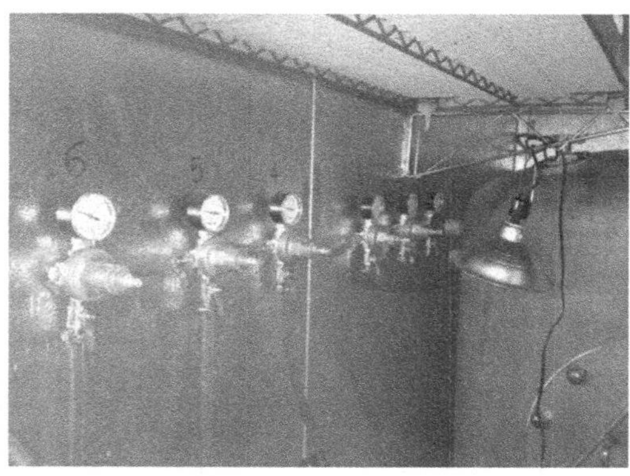

Cold Room Regulators

Chapter 10

HIRING YOUR STAFF

Don't wait until the last minute to let the public know that you will be hiring. While under construction display a large sign in the window explaining your brewery to the public. This sign should also let potential employees know how they can get in touch with you for interviews. During the early days of construction, you will just take their names and phone numbers. Keep applications on hand to give applicants. I just use the basic ones available at any office supply store, or you can make up your own. As opening day approaches you can get in touch with them.

When you actually start to advertise for help, accept applications at specific times, say on Thursdays from 3:00 – 4:00 PM. That way you will not be constantly interrupted with applicants while you are in the final crunch days of construction. By setting aside specific times, it allows you to give your undivided attention to the prospective employee.

Non-Negotiable Sheet

A great way to start with a possible employee is to give them a Non-Negotiable Sheet before they fill out an application. This is something that the Disney Company does and I recommend.

The Non-Negotiable Sheet explains up front all the things about your business that you will hold the line on. It could include such things as hair that is only of a natural color (not green or blue), no pierced eyebrows, etc. It is whatever is important enough to you that you will not negotiate with the new employee. Then, if the employee agrees with the items listed on this paper, he or she can fill out an application.

This is not legally binding, but it is a nifty way to let this person know what your limits are with employee appearance. You are being up-front and honest in informing the potential employee how you feel about certain things in your business. Isn't that a better way to begin a relationship?

INTERVIEWS

General Questions

I like to have one of those small pads of sticky notes on hand when I conduct an interview. When the interview is over you can jot down some first impressions about the person and stick it on their application. This will help you remember the person when you are going over the applications. With a sticky note, it does not become part of their permanent record so you are free to write whatever you want.

When you set up your interview, have a list of questions prepared in advance. This will keep the process consistent with all applicants. You can always add questions that pop up based on their answers as you go along.

A good first question to ask is why they applied with you in the first place. If they have a sense of humor, they will use it at this point. If they are sincere, they will tell you the truth. If they aren't sure, they will shrug their shoulders and say they don't know. Here are some other questions to ask:

- What is your ideal work schedule?
- When can you absolutely not work?
- Do you have any special needs we should know about, disabilities, etc.?

Specific Questions

Next, you delve into an area that will give you a little insight into what the person is like and how they may fit into your brewery.

- Explain why you are qualified for this job?
- Tell me about your last job and why you left?
- Describe the best job you have had?
- Describe your work ethic and your work habits?
- Do you have any ambitions in this business?

Thank them for their time and tell them that you will call in a specific period of time and let them know whether they have been hired.

Check References

After you interview, you will want to check the employee's references. It is amazing how few businesses look at references. You could argue that employees' won't list bad references, but in my experience, that isn't usually the case.

We once had a manager who took off to Hawaii with the weekend deposit. He was eventually caught and the insurance company made a deal with him not to prosecute if he returned the money. About two years later, we received a call from an employer checking on his references. We couldn't believe it; he actually put us down as a reference! We couldn't tell the person checking references that the guy was a thief, but we could say that he was not eligible for rehire.

Reference Questions

Here are some other good questions to ask when checking references:

- How long did this person work for you?
- How well did they get along with your managers and employees?
- Did this person follow instructions?
- Were they able to work independently?
- Were they able to handle stressful situations?

If the references make you feel comfortable, call the employee to let them know they have a job and to come in and fill out the paperwork. If it doesn't work out, then call them anyway and tell them that the job has been filled. Let them know that you appreciate their application and wish them well. Remember, you still want them as a customer and want no ill feeling from them. This small amount of work will pay dividends in the future.

After I sold Il Vicino Wood Oven Pizza & Brewery to my partners, my wife and I moved out to San Francisco for a sabbatical. I thought it would be fun to brew while I was there and sent my resume to ten different breweries in the area. I received one response and it was from Fritz Maytag, owner of Anchor Brewing. While he didn't have anything for me, at least he responded and wished me luck.

To this day, Anchor Steam is part of my beer selection. The people you do not hire can also become good customers, so show them the respect they are due and call them to let them know you will not be hiring them.

New Employee Paperwork

Now that you've hired this employee, there is a certain amount of paperwork they must fill out. Start an employee file with their name on the front and all the paperwork that the government requires them to have inside the file.

In the U.S. this will be a W-4 and an I-9. In Canada, the employee will give you their social security number, a T-4, and fill out a Canadian pension form.

In addition to this, you will want to give them an employee manual, job description, training checklist, and any other information that they will need. Blank folders should be made up ahead of time so that when you hire a new employee, you're ready to go. The I-9 and W-4 are filled out and given back along with the folder. The employee keeps all the other information pertaining to his or her job. Next, you write the employee's name on the folder and it goes into you employee files. Employee evaluations and raise information can be added later for future reference.

Once you have the new employee in front of you, take the time to go through the paper work with them. As things get rolling, you may not have time later. If you take the time now, you can be assured that the employee knows what's expected of them. Go through the employee manual you have put together and also the job descriptions. Answer any questions they have. What will come through is your enthusiasm for the brewery and that will be infectious. In addition, they will not be able to use the excuse that they were not informed.

This paperwork process takes about fifteen to thirty minutes, but it is time well spent. First impressions mean something, and when the new employee sees you take such a keen interest right from the beginning, they will subconsciously know that their job is very important to you. When you are finished, take the new employee on a tour to explain where everything is such as parking, the employee break area, etc.

Chapter 11

TRAINING

Brad Smith comes to work at the brewery as a bartender. He has already filled out his paper work, taken a tour, and clocked in. On his first day on the job he is assigned a trainer. This is someone who knows the job well and is paid a small premium to train new employees. The trainer receives a training checklist from you and takes a few minutes to go over some of the simple things on the list with Brad. These would include where to park, the phone number, hours of operation, and what credit cards are accepted.

Brad and his trainer spend the rest of the day performing the job while using the training checklist as a reference. At the end of the shift, the trainer goes back through the checklist and quizzes Brad on all of the items covered. The trainer explains to Brad that he will not be able to work on his own until he can pass a small written test covering the items on the training check list.

Brad is scheduled to train for two more days. On each day he will be with a trainer (perhaps not the same trainer), and trained on the same checklist. By going over the same list every day, and being quizzed on the same material, it is more likely that Brad will learn it. At the end of his third day, he sits down and takes a short written test. If he passes, he is on the schedule by himself. If he fails, he gets another day of training, followed by another test.

BARTENDER TRAINING CHECK LIST

__PHONE NUMBER AND ADDRESS
__DIRECTIONS TO BREWERY
__TELEPHONE ANSWERING AND OPERATION
__EMPLOYEE PARKING
__BREAKS, PAY PERIODS, SCHEDULES
__UNIFORM
__EMPLOYEE DISCOUNTS
__MICROS OPERATIONS
__CREDIT CARD MACHINE
__RESTROOM CLEANING
__TRASH AND RECYCLING
__FLOOR MOPPING
__DAILY CHECKLIST
__BEER POURING
__CHANGING KEGS
__BREWING PROCESS
__SERVICE SYSTEM
__GROWLER FILLS AND RETURNS
__KEG SALES AND DEPOSITS
__INTOXICATED CUSTOMERS AND CUT-OFFS
__PROMOS

EMPLOYEE________________________________
TRAINER_________________________________
DATE____________________

BARTENDER TEST

1. What is the telephone number and address?
2. On the back page, draw a map showing directions and location.
3. Briefly explain the brewing process.
4. List the beers on tap and describe them.

Develop training checklists for each position in your brewery. You can start blank folders for each position and then inside each folder put an I-9 and W-4 form, employee manual if you use one, and your training checklists. That way when you hire a new employee you are ready to go. Put the name of the employee on the folder and as the employee fills out paper work, employee training checklists and tests they go back in the folder and become part of the employees permanent record. Slick.

TRAINING WEEK

The first day of staff training, follow your training checklist. You would be surprised to know how many businesses go through the expense of building their brewery, only to fall short by not spending the appropriate amount of time training their staff. For them opening day arrives and the staff does not know how to handle the many situations that arise. The following system works, trust me.

Pre-Opening Schedule

It is wise to open on a Monday, which is usually a slower day. This will give your employees and yourself a little adjustment time. However, the process of opening will actually begin on a Saturday, nine days before your official opening day.

Saturday

Have a meeting with all new employees to discuss the schedule of events for opening. This will include training, and times different people will arrive for their specific training. Make the meeting upbeat and be well prepared. Definitely have coffee made and something to eat for everyone. Introduce yourself and any other managers and explain what the brewery is about.

If the group is small enough, have people introduce themselves as well. Keep the meeting short. No need to get long-winded about finally achieving your dream. Once everyone has their schedules, thank them for coming and tell them you will see them on Monday.

Sunday

This will be the quiet before the storm. You may want to have a couple of people from the Saturday meeting do a final cleaning, put away stock, or other last minute chores. However, try to get out of there at a reasonable time. Go home and rest up for the coming week.

Monday

Don't have your people come in at the same time. Have everyone divided by job description, and, if it is a large group, divided again into small groups. For example, if you have six bar/servers, have a group "A" consisting of three people come in at one time and a group "B" at another. That way you can work with a smaller number and it is easier for them to be involved.

Teach the servers the proper way to pour a pint, change a keg and fill a growler. Also, go over how to greet people, cleaning techniques, the checklist system, and how the service system will work. Have them each take a turn on the register ringing up fictitious orders to build speed.

If they have cooking duties, you may want to have group "B" working in the kitchen while group "A" is working at the bar then switch them. If you have separate kitchen people, they also will be divided into groups.

Your goal by the end of the day will be for the groups to further divide and serve each other. Do this a few times and at the end of the day have a meeting with everyone to discuss how things went. It will be rough, I guarantee it, but you will learn valuable things about how you set the brewery up. If the placement of certain pieces of equipment doesn't work, you can change it before you are open to the public. Or, if the flow at the cash register causes a bottleneck you hadn't expected, you have the opportunity to change the location of the register or add another one.

Tuesday

Use this day the same way you did Monday's session. You may want to switch the times you are working with the groups. Today your employees will have a little better idea of what is going on and you will find it much easier. The important part of the day other than the repeating of the training will be when everyone serves each other.

At the end of the day, have a quick meeting to discuss what went right and what still needs improving. Your employees will see improvements you can make in small areas that you have not seen. Finally, ask your employees to have some of their friends or relatives come in for free beer and food on Wednesday evening. Give them specific times to come and limit the amount of people coming.

Wednesday

You are going to go through the exact training protocols you established on Monday and Tuesday. Through repetition, you can pick out potential trouble spots in the system, or employees.

Wednesday is a dress rehearsal day. Your goal is to serve people who have never been in before – the friends and relatives of your employees. Keep the number of people invited to a manageable size, no more than 30. Things may have been smooth the day before, but for some reason as soon as your new customers come in, things will start to break down. Don't be alarmed. This is how everyone learns. Your customers won't mind as it didn't cost them anything and they feel like they are a part of the business and want to help. Following the pattern, finish this day with a meeting to discuss what went right and what didn't. The next day gets a little more serious.

Thursday

The goal today is to start serving people who you don't know. Invite people from around your business community, those in offices or neighborhoods who may likely be your customers anyway. Go door to door and hand them an invitation with a specific time on it. Stagger these times so that everyone doesn't come at once. It is likely that invited guests will not show up exactly as you asked them to. Be mentally prepared to have the excitement of a lot of people coming at the same time.

Try to find people who will be enthusiastic about the brewery. Choose people who are leaders in their circle of friends. If you win them over, they will tell many more people, than the shy people who keep to themselves.

Much of the training has been done with three days of repetitive duties. Treat this as a normal shift with employees coming in and going through their normal set-up duties.

You should position yourself at the door to greet your guests and explain that this is all for training and that you would appreciate any suggestions they may offer. Give them a customer comment card and ask them to fill it out at the end of their visit and leave it on the table. Tell them how much you appreciate them coming to help you prepare for a smooth opening.

You also need to be at the door to keep out all the other people who want to come in because they think you are open. If you want, you can let some of them in to turn up the volume on the training. Once again, have a meeting at the end of the shift to go over the comment cards and discuss the day.

Friday

Today is just like Thursday. Do everything the same only with the improvements you made since the day before. You will want to mix up your employees so they get the most experience possible. Your goal today however is a smooth shift. After a long week, it should start to feel pretty comfortable. The crew should have some confidence and know what they are doing. They won't be perfect at their jobs, as they have only been working for one week, however, they will be better than they were on Monday. Hopefully your comment cards will reflect this.

Saturday

Have a party! Make a separate invitation for this. Throw a grand opening party and set times for it to begin and especially for it to end. I like having the hours from 5:00 PM to 8:00 PM. Decide what you want to serve like samples of food items on your menu, and have some of your employees there to help serve and clean up.

Invite all your family and friends, the construction crew, the bankers, lawyers, accountants, me, and especially all the neighbors and people who have been coming the nights before. Pack the place! Make it fun and above all, make it short.

Even though it is your brewery, stay sober. The mood will be to cut loose and have a good time, but someone needs to keep an eye on everyone so that they do not get too inebriated, and to make sure there is no damage to your brewery from a wild party. Sorry to tell you this, but it's you.

Stay at the door to greet people and to keep out the freeloaders. Let everyone know that you will be officially open for business on Monday and ask people to come back! It is always a good idea to ask people for their business.

Sunday

Sleep in. Rest. Read the paper, then go into work and take a moment to enjoy the quiet. You are about to open and you are sitting in your brewery. You can use this day to make sure you have everything ready for your first day of business. Do what you need to do then get out of there and enjoy a quiet rest of the day with family or friends, or just keep to yourself and go to bed early.

Over the last week, you have spent a great deal of money on inventory and on wages. However, you may have noticed that I didn't suggest you take out any ads in newspapers or radio. If I had, you would have spent a whole lot more.

This week you spent a few thousand dollars, but you gained far more. Not only have you trained your employees well, you engaged a lot of potential customers, fed them, and made them feel that they are a part of your business. This in effect, makes them goodwill ambassadors in the community. This is how word of mouth spreads. All the "experts" say this is the best form of advertising, and I agree.

The bonus to opening this way is your employee's also receive the best kind of training because they had a chance to pour a lot of beer and serve real customers. You are now ready to start your brewery with a well-trained staff and a good core customer base. Not a bad start. Now it's time to open!

STEP 3
THE BUSINESS SYSTEM

Chapter 12

WHAT MAKES IT GO

Before you can open, you need to have all the elements of your business system in place. No matter what type of food you serve, or if you are just packaging, or any other variation of brewery you intend to open, the following system can be integrated.

It simply is not good enough to have excellent beer and service to be profitable. You need a good business system to manage your day-to-day operation and deliver a predictable result. Even if you are super creative and change things around all the time, you need to do so within a framework that keeps the original idea in focus. This step is one of the most important in the whole process. You will see it all revolves around checklists. Everyone gets at least one.

Check Lists

My old partners would tease me about wanting a checklist for everything as though brushing my teeth was on my morning checklist. The truth is if you want something done consistently, you need a daily reminder.

Memory is not that consistent. If it is consistency you are after, then use a checklist. You need to follow a checklist just to remind you of all the small details that are essential to running your business. Even if you had no employees, you need something that is an anchor of duties for your business. You cannot count on your memory, and you sure cannot count on your moods.

In fact, running a brewery based on how you feel on any particular day is a formula for disaster! You need a system that is above moods and memory. A simple list of things to do on any given day is one of the most powerful business tools available to you. If you closed this book right now and made a daily checklist for yourself, and followed it, you would have made a great impact on your business. But don't close this book; we've only just started.

Checklists are for anybody who performs work in your brewery. If you were a sole proprietor, you would operate off a pretty substantial list, as you would be the one who does everything. However as you grow and hire new employees, you will want some sort of list for them to follow. In fact, it actually gets easier with this system when you have more employees, you can divvy up the duties that need to be done. You'll see what I mean as we progress.

One of our first restaurants had nearly one hundred employees. What a headache! When we started we used only bare bones checklists, which revolved more around opening and closing duties. As time went on it became obvious that we needed to commit more detail to paper and try to spread the workload out among more employees, everyone from dishwasher to management. We looked at larger restaurant chains and other businesses to see how they dealt with this issue. Besides for some impressive training systems, they all had terrific checklists. Every successful business we looked at had an excellent checklist system. This all seems obvious to me now, but back then it was revolutionary.

Identify Brewery Positions

First of all, you need to identify all the positions in your business. Not how many employees you have, but what the actual positions are. Employees move around in positions, but the positions themselves stay pretty much the same. If you have someone who is the principal bartender, then that is a position. Someone whose main focus is cleaning kegs would also be considered to be in a separate position. The same goes for cooks and dishwashers if you have them.

As your business grows, you may add positions such as assistant manager, bus person, and so on. Many of your employees will learn more than one position, it's important to make up the checklists for the positions and not for the individuals in those positions.

For a 50-seat brewpub, serving a limited menu, you would probably have the following positions.

Manager
Bartender
Wait Person
Cook
Dishwasher
Brewer
Assistant Brewer

The Perfect Employee

Now that you have decided how many checklists you need, what are you going to put on them? You could start by writing all the things that particular position should do, but I have a loftier goal in mind. I suggest you start by asking yourself what the perfect employee would do in this position.

For example, make a list of all the things you would like the bartender to do in a shift. Now picture this supreme bartender-of-all-time in that position and ask yourself, "what tasks would make this employee so great?" This perspective adds a different slant into making up simple checklists. It lets you see more possibilities and new ways to improve your business.

Here is the bartender checklist we use at Colorado Boy.

Opening Duties

Sign in on Micros
Turn heat to 70
Sweep and mop floor
Wipe down bar trash can
Wipe down tables & chairs, sills and ledge tops with Simple Green or Pledge
Set up tables and chairs with menus and red pepper shakers
Clean bathroom mirror, toilet, and trash-cans. Restock paper & soap
Set up popcorn area and make popcorn
Wipe down inside and top of bar refrigerator
Restock wine (two of each on shelf and in fridge)
Set lights and music
Turn on outside light and beer menu light
Plug in beer tower fan
Check beer supply & beer gas
Turn on panini press and set up oil & brush
Bring up bread from freezer if needed & bring sandwiches to par
Count bar bank
Do side duties

Turn Open sign

Side Duties

MON-Pledge wine bottle shelf, dust wine bottles, put out trash
TUES- Clean tables/bar & bar front panels/ furniture/sills with pledge
WED-Clean bar & brewery mirrors. Clean shelves under bar
THU-Clean inside & out of front door. Sweep bricks around doorway
FRI-Scrub bar hand sink, pledge back bar and cabinets
SAT-Clean legs of chairs, bar stools, dust cove base
SUN-Polish beer tower with Brasso. Use paper towels

Closing Duties

Pull glasses, clean shelf matting, clean marble
Spray rubber mats, place in brewery
Pump air out of wine bottles
Wipe bar, tables, and menus
Wipe tap handles
Wipe out bar drains and sinks
Sweep floors, bathroom, kitchen, and bar room
Do dirty dishes
Seal food containers and wipe clean sandwich prep table
Clean popcorn machine and bowls
Turn off panini press and clean. Wipe down tables
Empty kitchen, bathroom, and brewery trash, replace trash bags
Unplug beer tower, turn off light in walk-in
Put up chairs and stools
Ring out credit cards and micros sales

Turn off music system
Do daily books
Turn heater to 55
Turn off menu board light and outside light
Turn off all lights and fans and outside door light
Sign out on micros
Lock-up

Manager Checklists

The checklist for the manager is just as important, if not more important, than the one you made for each of your employees. It makes a difference when the manager comes to work in the morning and can grab his or her list on a clipboard, going through all the reminders of the different tasks that need to be done on a daily basis.

Some can be as simple as a reminder to check the employee schedule to see who is coming in for the day. This step can avoid a problem if there was a scheduling mistake and you are short a person. The manager can also put the deposit together for the bank, pick the sandwich or beer specials for the day, and set the lights and music before opening.

There are certain things you need on the list that provide a redundancy to the items that are on the employee lists. For example, the employee may have as a last item on their list to be checked out by a manager, and your list will have a reminder to check out the employees. This way, it is less likely that this important job will be forgotten. You can also add things like a walk through inspection before you open to make sure things like the open sign is on, or that the flowers outside your front door are healthy, watered, and not full of cigarette butts.

By the way, this is a good place to mention that it is best to have an employee smoking and/or break area away from where your customers see them. Smoking is looked upon as an unclean habit and can give a negative impression to your customers.

Here are some suggestions for things to include on your manager checklist:

AM

____ Check Schedule
____ Check GM Book
____ Count Change Bank
____ Do Deposit
____ Check In Deliveries
____ Set Lights And Music
____ Do Pre-Opening Walk Through
____ Talk To Customers
____ Monitor Floor Activities
____ Check Out Employees
____ Write In Log Book
____ Count AM Cash Drawer
____ Meet With PM Manager

PM

____ Check Schedule
____ Check Scoreboard (more on this later)
____ Walk Through
____ Monitor Floor Activities
____ Check Out Employees
____ Ring Out Registers
____ Run Credit Card Machine
____ Write In Log Book

____ Turn Off All Lights. Make Sure Back Door Is Locked
____ Set Alarm

The General Maintenance (GM) Book

Along with the checklists for all of your employees and managers, there are some things that do not need to be done on a daily basis. These reminders need to be tied more to a calendar than to the week. Perhaps things that needs to be done every other week or once a month. This is where we use what we'll call a GM Book, GM for "General Maintenance".

How to Create a GM Book

To make a GM book, you will need to get a three ring binder and 31 tab dividers from your local office supply store. In between each tab divider, you need a piece of paper that you will be the reminders you need - usually just one piece of paper that you will write on in between the tabs. This doesn't have to be anything fancy. Just write down things you will want to remember.

For example, you might have reminders to pay certain taxes that are due by a given date. Or, you may insert a reminder that on the 25th of the month, the Chamber of Commerce puts out its monthly calendar of upcoming conventions that could affect your business.

The GM book is also great for handling maintenance concerns. For instance, cleaning the screens of the compressors on all your refrigeration at least twice a month. Write this on the 13th and the 28th. This can save you a lot of cash by not having to replace a compressor that overheated because of dirty compressor screens.

We discussed the manager's daily checklist. One of the items on that list was to check the GM book. The GM book won't do you any good unless you remember to pick it up every day and look at it. The manager's daily checklist reminds you to do that.

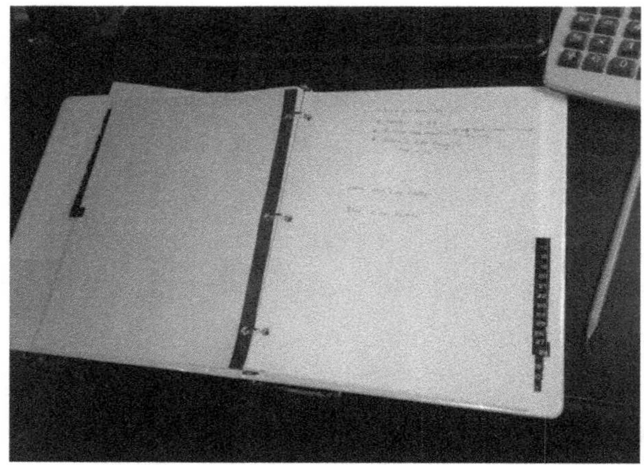

GM Book

There may be days when the brewery is hectic and you just can't get to the GM book. Other days you may be swimming in free time and you can get a week's worth of GM book duties done. Nothing is set in stone. This is just a simple system to remember all the little things that will make your brewery run smoothly.

The Repair & Maintenance (R&M) Book

Your brewery will have repair and maintenance issues. A brewpub, in particular has a lot of customer traffic going through it on a daily basis, as well as restaurant equipment that can be abused by your employees, not to mention brewing equipment. When things break, they usually break on a Saturday or Sunday when it costs more to have it repaired. Or it may break during the busiest times. The best way to deal with problems as they come up is to have a good tool at your disposal and I'm not talking about a wrench or a screwdriver.

Some of the equipment in your brewery will come with a manual. Keep these manuals in a safe place – preferably an equipment file so that you can refer to them for any replacement parts that you may need. The manuals will also be a great help in preparing your R&M Book as each piece of equipment will have its own maintenance needs.

How to Create the R&M Book

The R&M book is not something that you check every day like the GM book, but rat her a quick reference guide to use in emergencies. Consult this book before you call in a professional on emergencies such as a locked up cash register, a dripping faucet, or a warm refrigerator.

It takes time to build a good R&M book that is customized for your brewery. To begin, look at all the things that could need repair and find out ahead of time what you can do yourself to fix it.

In a notebook, create chapters relating to that piece of equipment. List the problem, probable cause, and how to fix it. For example, the lights don't work in a part of the tasting room. Before you call an electrician, you go to your handy R&M book and look under:

Lighting

Problem Lights not turning on
Probable Cause tripped circuit breaker
Repair/Reset the breaker

Then you go to the breaker box and reset the breaker. Sounds simple, but if you asked an electrician how often they are called for a tripped breaker, you would be amazed at the number.

Leaky Faucet

Another simple one is a leaky faucet. Sooner or later, all faucets start to leak because of minerals in the water. Once the dripping starts, it wastes a lot of water and energy. To the customer, it says something subconsciously about the way you run your business. Many people would call a plumber. Before you call a plumber, you go to your handy R&M book and look under:

Problem Leaky faucet
Probable CauseBad gasket
Repair Replace Gasket

The job takes about five satisfying minutes and costs you about twenty cents (the cost of the gasket) to fix.

Building Your R&M Book

The way you build this book is to list all the things you think could break down in your brewery. Next, talk to some of your handy friends or better yet, professionals, and ask them how the problem could be fixed. In the case of the faucet, you would find out what size gaskets belong in all your fixtures, and then go out and buy a supply of them.

Knowing that your cash register will most likely lock up at some point, you would talk to a technician to find out ways to reset the machine to get it to work again. If that fails, you would have a backup plan in your book that would involve a calculator and some hand written checks.

It takes time to build this book. You may only have a few repairs listed at first. However, when something breaks that you don't have the answer for, you will have to call in a professional to fix it. When that happens, you are presented with a golden opportunity to see how the problem was fixed and add that to your book. You might as well ask the professional a lot of other repair questions while they are at your place since you are paying for their time anyway.

As your business matures, so will your R&M book. It will be immensely helpful when you are away and it is up to your assistants to make the decision to fix something or call in a professional. Over time, you can imagine how much money this proactive book can save you.

Chapter 13

DOING THE BOOKS

The first thing to do in your brewery bookkeeping is to create a Change Bank. This is a box you keep in your safe with a specific amount of money in it. We use $400. It is divided into change from five-dollar bills down to pennies. It can be used for petty cash and to make change during a busy night when the first customer wants to pay with a $100 bill.

The next step involves doing the daily books. To do this we use what is called a Daily Sales Report.

The ownership of a brewery means selling beer, and that means taking in money. Just as important as the quality of your beer, is keeping track of how that money comes in and goes out. A good bookkeeping system is at the heart of a good business.

The simplest way to do the books would be to take all your sales for the day, make up a deposit slip and take it to the bank. However, if you did this, and many businesses do, in the long run you would be making your life more difficult. This is because you are selling much more than beer.

You are probably going to be selling food, perhaps liquor or wine, and maybe some merchandise, such as hats, tee shirts, and pint glasses.

Don't forget that depending on where you live, you may be collecting a sales tax too. All these types of sales should be kept track of in their own categories.

To maintain a food cost of say 30%, you will need to know how much of your sales came exclusively from food. The same goes for beer, wine, or merchandise. Here is a simple system to do just this. This will also integrate into some pretty exciting things that will help you be successful. However let's first look at the Daily Sales Report or DSR. A template appears on the next page, which you can change to suit your needs. The template is followed by an explanation of how to create a DSR.

DAILY SALES	TODAY__/__/__	MTD
BEER		
BEVERAGE		
WINE		
FOOD		
MERCH.		
TAX		
TOTAL		
CASH		
CHECKS		
CREDIT CARDS		
TOTAL		
OVER/SHORT		
Bartender________	PACE____/_____	=__________
Labor	__________	__________

How to Create a Daily Sales Report (DSR)

The DSR is simply your bookkeeping checklist. A piece of paper with lines on it to divide the categories of sales and the categories of money you bring in. Then a balance of the two resulting in an over, short, or even (balance) at the bottom of the ledger.

1. You will start by ringing out your cash register.
2. There will be a way for you to read your totals without resetting it back to zero, which can be done at any time, and a way to read the totals and reset the register for the next day.
3. Depending on the type of cash register you have, the register will print up your totals according to what categories you have set up. Let's assume it prints totals for Beer, Beverage, Wine, Food and Merchandise. It will also give you a total for tax collected, if there is sales tax where you live.
4. You will transfer those totals to the top portion of your DSR.
5. Next, you will count the money in your cash register drawer.
6. You do not start your day with an empty drawer because you would be unable to make change. So let's assume you start with $150 made up of change and bills, nothing larger than a five-dollar bill.
7. Separate the cash from the checks and the credit card receipts. Start counting the cash with a calculator that prints, beginning with the largest denominations down to the pennies. Make an entry into the calculator for every level of denomination. For example, count all the twenties and enter the amount, followed by the tens, and so forth.
8. When you have a total, subtract out the original $150, and then enter that into the DSR where it says " Cash".

9. Next, look at the tape from the calculator and add back the amounts starting this time with the pennies, on up to the fives. Take this amount and subtract it from $150 and the result will be what you need to add or subtract to your cash drawer to bring the drawer back to the original $150 it started with. The left over money will go into your deposit.
10. Then total the checks and enter that amount.
11. When you close out your credit card machine (your credit card company will show you how this works) it will print up a total of the credit cards for the day. Record that amount on your DSR and save the credit card receipts in a separate place for future reference. I like to just staple them to the back of the DSR. That way we have everything relating to that day in one place.
12. Finally, you will add all the types of revenue you collected, Cash, Checks, and Credit Cards to come up with a total. That total should match your total sales for the day. If there is a difference, that is written down into your over/short space.

Correcting Errors

What if it doesn't match? Mistakes can happen in many places. The first place to look, however, will be within your "money triangle." It is made up of three areas where you have money:

1. **Your change bank** (let's assume it to be $400)
2. **Your cash drawer** (we said it was $150)
3. **Your deposit** (your sales for the day)

If you are short in your deposit, you must be over in one of the other two areas. For example, if you finish your deposit and then re-count your change bank and find that it is $20 short, most likely you are

$20 over in your deposit or your cash drawer. The remedy would be to re-count those to locate the missing $20.

The exception to this would be a mistake at the cash register. This would include things like giving the wrong change, or forgetting to adjust for a mistaken item rung up. To find these mistakes is a lot tougher. However, if you look first to the money triangle, you will find the majority of your mistakes.

How to Make Fewer Errors

To assure that there are fewer mistakes when you do your books, always start the process by counting your change bank and end the process the same way. When I count a change bank, I make it a habit to run a calculator tape. Next to the total I put the date and my initials on it.

It's sort of like my guarantee that there is that amount of money in there. I place the tape in the change bank with the money. The next time the money is counted, whoever is doing the counting knows when it was counted last and that it had the correct amount of money in it.

Recording Your Pace

At the very bottom of your DSR, there is a place to record your pace. Your pace is an estimate of what you hope to do in sales in any given time – for our example, one month – based on the sales you have done so far in the month. It is based on a fraction, as in 5/31, in other words 5 days out of 31.

As an easy example, let's say that at the end of day 5 you have done $5,000. Using this formula, you would take the total sales month to date ($5,000), and divide it by the number of days of business so far in that month ($5,000 divided by 5). This gives you average daily sales of

$1,000. Now take that average daily sales figure and multiply it by the total number of days in the month ($1,000 times 31) and this will give you a total of $31,000.

Assuming you continue to average $1,000 per day, you will have a pretty good idea of how much in sales you will do for the month. Stay with me here, this is powerful stuff. Instead of waiting until the end of the month to see how well you did, you will know on a daily basis. Armed with this information, you can now make adjustments in labor or start new promotions to boost sales. As we will get into later, this works into the budget process so that you can plan your profits instead of just hoping for the best.

When you are finished doing your books, take the print-out from the cash register that you used to record your sales information, and tape it to the back of your DSR. This will give you a way to verify that the sales you recorded on your DSR are the same as the sales recorded on your cash register. This will come in to play when you do your audits, which will be explained later in this manual.

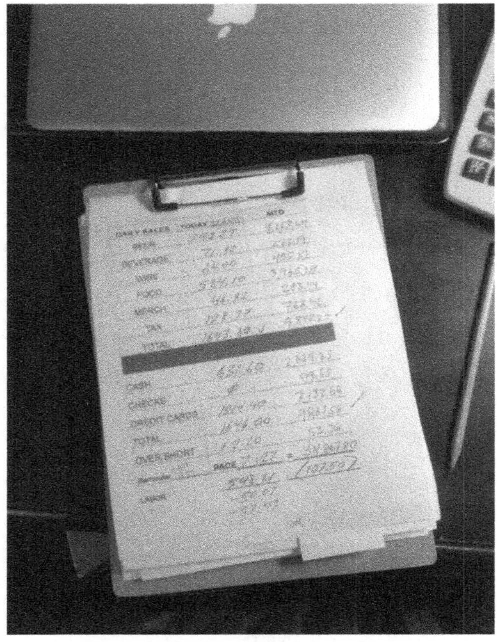

Daily Sales Register (DSR)

Budgets

Sooner or later, you probably figured we would come around to budgets. They are central to the whole system, as are checklists. For most of us, being in business is about being our own boss, having fun, AND making a profit. I suppose there are a few folks out there that go into business just for something to do. I would guess that if they were not concerned about making a profit, they would not remain in business long. Profit helps define the difference between success and failure, financially speaking.

Profit is not a dirty word. If you don't make a profit, you cannot pay yourself or your employees, let alone give raises and benefits. If you are not making a profit, you will have a hard time keeping up with the maintenance of your brewery and it will start to fall apart. You can't afford to advertise so business continues to drop off. You didn't get into business to fail. If you really want to succeed, you need all the tools you can get in order to achieve success.

Budgets are one of the most effective tools for success. Can you name one successful company that does not budget? With budgets you have more control of the cash going OUT of your business. Remember, "It's not how much you make, but how much you keep".

When we started our first restaurant, we would go through our month making deposits, doing our inventories, and taking care of our customers. Then, at the end of the month we would put all of our monthly financial information together and send it off to our accountant. He would get the information by the 7th of the month, then do his part and get it back to us in the form of a Profit and Loss Statement (P&L) usually by the 15th.

You see the problem with this system is that the information is already so old it doesn't do a whole lot of good. If it showed that we didn't make any money, that month is already history. In fact, the current month is already half over. What we needed was information in real time. We needed a P&L at the BEGINNING of the month. We call this P&L a budget!

Profit & Loss (P&L) Statement

What you will do at the beginning of your month is to create the P&L that you would like to see. This will tell you what your sales are, the cost of sales, and all your expenses (to the best of your knowledge). Then you try to make this a reality by working your system every day.

Believe me, it's much more likely to happen if you start down this road at the beginning of the month with a road map. Your budget is your road map; your P&L. Here's how you do it.

Prioritize

A P&L is laid out for you like a priority list. The items on the list are:

#1 Sales

Without sales, you cannot stay in business. Money coming in is the fuel for the machine. By working on promoting your business, providing value to the customer and so on, you develop your sales potential.

#2 Cost of Sales

How much do you spend on the raw product that makes up what you are selling? The cost of sales is just the total of what you spent for the things you actually sell, such as grain and hops, or bottles of wine, or the groceries used to prepare the food on your menu. It is not what you spent for utilities, insurance, repairs, etc.

#3 Labor

You still have a long way to go on the list before you get to net profit. As far as expenses go, labor is the biggest behind the raw products you are selling. Therefor keeping labor costs down is essential to keeping profits up!

80/20 Principal

An Italian mathematician Vilfredo Perato (1848-1923) came up with what is now referred to the 80/20 principal. Basically it states that 80% of your results come from 20% of your effort. Translated into a P&L it means that by concentrating on Sales, Cost of Sales, and Labor, you will produce the majority of your profit. It's a pretty simple concept.

For example, if you had just one extra hour a week to spend on your brewery, would it be better spent on coming up with a new sales promotion, or researching a different style of trash bag to purchase that is less expensive? In other words, the one-hour spent on sales could bring in an extra $1,000 for the month, while the trash bag savings – while important – would only save you $25!

If your focus is not on sales, then go down the list. How about a new menu item to sell that would yield a better food cost or a new way to schedule that could save a couple of labor hours a day?

By prioritizing your precious time and applying the 80/20 principal, you will go farther and faster. The inverse is to spend all your time working on items that are very low on your P&L. We are always concentrating our effort on what will bring our business the greatest good, for the least amount of effort. Once we understand this, it will make building a budget more meaningful. Let's look a little closer at our P&L to better understand the impact of this priority list.

Managing Sales

Sales are the foundation of any business. Remember, "No sales, no business." So how do we manage sales? One way is to quantify it.

The longer you are in business, the more data you will collect. This includes keeping track of your sales figures. After you have a full year under your belt, it will become easier to predict your sales for the current year. This will help you to know if your sales are growing or shrinking.

Comparing sales to the prior month isn't really accurate enough because sales fluctuate throughout the year. This is based on seasonal trends like summer break, Christmas, tax time, etc. You can't really estimate what January is going to be like until you have experienced a January. It certainly isn't going to be like December, when the hordes are out shopping, dining and drinking.

To find out what your sales are going to be, interview other business owners and find out what their busy times of the year are. Once you have a month or two of sales, you can best judge if the next month will be busier or slower depending on what you learned from other businesses. All this becomes so much easier once you have a whole year's worth of sales to look back on. After you have reached this milestone, it will be a breeze to create your budget.

Sales

The first item on our budget is sales. You'll want to look at the prior year's sales for the month, and then look at the trends of the current year. Are your sales up from last year an average of 5%? If so, add 5% to what you predict you will do in sales for the current month. You can then make any other adjustments, such as construction on the street in front of your brewery, or a large convention in town bringing in lots of extra business.

Other factors to look at are things like the calendar. How many weekends in the month will affect your business. Special holidays or long weekends can add or subtract from your sales.

The system we are building here for your brewery will make it easier to build these budgets as your business matures.

Cost of Sales & Inventory

First, you need to know what the things you sell are costing you. If you are unclear on how to calculate this, we need to figure this out. The best way to do this is with an inventory. This is a necessary evil. Many business owners get into trouble because they do not keep track of their inventories. How can you hope to stay in business if you don't have a firm grip on what you are selling? It's all about inventory control. Next to sales, it is the most important thing you can focus on in your business. Let's look at how you will work with your inventory and your sales.

Cost of Sales

To calculate cost of sales you use the following formula:

Beginning inventory, plus purchases, minus ending inventory, equals cost of sales.

Let's look at a simple example. Say you started the month out with a case of beer (24 bottles at $1 each). The values of your "beginning inventory" would be $24. Then during the month you purchase another two cases. That would be $48. Then at the end of the month you do an inventory and you have 18 bottles left, or, $18 in value. Using the above formula, $24 + $48 - $18 = $54 - so far so good. This means you sold 54 bottles of beer because each beer is worth $1. Looking at your DSR for the month you see that your beer sales were $162. You divide your Cost of Sales number ($54) by your Sales number (162) and it equals your PC (percent cost) 33.33%

With beer you are not only selling finished product like kegs, bottles, and beer in tanks, you are essentially also selling the ingredients that you use to make beer like grain and hops. So these things also have to be included in your inventory. You need to place a value of everything you have in inventory so that you can divide that value by your total sales to see what your PC is.

The first thing you do is to establish a beginning inventory. Take inventory on the first day of the month. To do this you will need to inventory all the things you sell, such as grain, hops, and finished beer etc., and then multiply each item by what the item costs per unit (your cost). Next, add the columns to come up with a total value of the inventory. This will give you your current inventory in dollars.

Date___________

Beer Inventory

Hand Count	**Malt**	**Amount**	**Price**	**Total**
________	2 Row	1000	0.68	680
________	40 L	0	0.9	0
________	60L	54	0.83	44.82
________	120 L	95	0.83	78.85
________	Carapils	125	0.79	98.75
________	Munich 10L	50	0.7	35
________		0	0.63	0
________	Chocolate	5	0.86	4.3
________	Ashburn	150	0.71	106.5
________	Victory	44	0.88	38.72
________	Extra Special	30	0.89	26.7
________	White Wheat	67	0.77	51.59
________		0	0.83	0
________	Black	21	0.83	17.43
________	Flaked Barley	0	0.48	0
________	Rice Hulls	0	0.58	0
________	Viena	23	0.7	16.1
________	Roasted Barley	2	0.83	1.66
			$	**1,200.42**
	Hops			
________	Liberty	1	24.5	24.5
________	US Challenger	15	23	345
________	Warrior	0.23	11	2.53
________	Arg. Cascade	22	22	484
________	US Cascade	12	12.35	148.2
________	UK Fuggle	8	11.55	92.4
________	Crystal	6	12.23	73.38
________	Centennial	54	10.12	546.48
________	Summit	39.5	14.4	568.8
		0	0	0
		0	0	0
			$	**2,285.29**
	Finished Product			
________	Guest Beers	0	90	0
________	Yeast	1	120	120
________	Cases	0	0	0
________	1/2 BBL's	7.7	22.5	173.25
________	1/4 BBL's	0	7.5	0
________	5 Gal	2	7.25	14.5
________	Tanks (BBL's)	17.08	45	768.6
________				
			$	**1,076.35**

Beginning Inventory	4837.7	
Purchases	1113.25	
Ending Inventory	$ 4,562.06	
Cost of Goods Sold	$ 1,388.89	
Sales	12515.79	
PC	**11.1%**	**30-Sep-2009**

Beer Inventory Sheet

This simple spreadsheet can be used for your hand count by filling in the numbers in the column to the left. Next type those numbers into the program. Your beginning inventory number is the ending inventory number from last month. You get your sales number and your purchases number from your Quickbooks or other accounting program. The spreadsheet will calculate your current PC (percentage cost) based on the numbers provided. You repeat this for everything you sell.

Sample Sales Breakdown:

- Beer
- Wine
- Food
- Merchandise

You would then have a separate inventory sheet for every one of these categories with all the inventory items that go with them. The total of all the categories will be your overall cost.

Why would you do your inventory this way compared to the easier way? Simple. It's about information and you can't manage it unless you can quantify it.

You will develop target percentages for each of these categories. If one of them is off, it is easier to look at that specific area for the problem rather than the problem being lost in all the things you sell. It's not any harder to do it this way.

These percentages are important for figuring your budget. If you guess that you are going to do $35,000 in sales, all you need to do to budget in your cost of sales is to multiply the sales figure by your current total food cost. This is how you plug in the second most important number in your budget!

Each category has its own inventory spreadsheet just like the example above. When printed out, the column on the left is used to physically write in the amounts. Then you will enter those amounts onto the spreadsheet on the computer in the "Amount" column. You will also need to update the prices of the inventory as they change. Some things, like produce, change almost weekly. Spices stay pretty consistent. Your inventory should have the most up-to-date prices as they reflect the current value of your inventory.

At the bottom of the spreadsheet are the calculations. You will use your last inventories Ending Inventory figure to be the current Beginning Inventory figure. You calculate the purchases by adding up all the invoices in between your last inventory and the one you are taking. The Sales figure is also calculated by adding up the sales from the last inventory to the current one.

Labor Costs

It is almost impossible to avoid labor costs. Even if it is just you in your business, you must pay yourself something! Outside of the products you actually purchase to sell (Cost of Goods Sold), it is your biggest expense. Every dollar you save here goes right to the bottom line and beyond.

Labor Formula by Percentage

There are two ways to figure out your labor. The first is a percentage. You calculate this by dividing the cost of labor for any given period; say a month, by sales in that same period. Let's say you spent $7,700 last month on wages. Your sales were $35,000 (taxes not included, they are not sales). You divide $7,700 by $35,000, which equals 22%. This means for every dollar you took in, it cost you .22 cents in labor. If you establish that your monthly labor cost is 22%, then you would multiply whatever number you hope to be your monthly sales in your budget by 22%. That will give you the total you can spend on labor.

Labor Formula by Actual Cost

Another way you can figure out your labor budget is to schedule based on the actual cost of the labor. You will know the minimum amount of people needed to operate your brewery and you just multiply their hours by what they make an hour. There will be a minimum number of labor hours needed, but there should also be a maximum as well. This will be reflected in varying labor percentages. If sales are low, then your labor cost will be high as a percentage. If your sales go through the roof, then it will reflect in a very low labor cost.

Schedule-based Approach

I prefer the schedule-based approach. This is a good starting point. If after you have created your budget and it looks like you are going to be in the red, then you can go back and change the schedule on your budget worksheet to try to cut hours by being more creative where you can. You do this before you actually post the schedule, that way assuring that you can afford to schedule the employees that you had planned.

Labor Saving Tips

Here are some ideas you can start off with to save you money on labor:

1. Alternating arrival and departure times for employees. Concentrate your labor during times when you have the most sales. Stagger the times your employees come to work, and when they leave. This puts the most employees on when it is the busiest.

2. Pay your best people a little more, but have them cover during slow times so that you can eliminate a person entirely. You could have one morning and one night with a third good employee that comes in a little later in the morning and works into the night shift through the busy times, instead of two morning people and two night people. It gives you the same coverage while eliminating one position.
3. Assign extra responsibilities to management. This includes small things that can be done in place of an extra person coming in to do them. For example our manager does the daily laundry (towels and aprons). Or, the manager can help with closing duties to get everyone off the clock earlier.
4. By using your checklist system, you can assign extra work to your core employees to cover for other employees, allowing them to come in later, or not at all.

Managing labor is one of the most critical things you can do for your brewery. It is also one of the most difficult, because your employees' paychecks are affected. This is a situation where you keep individuals in mind as well as the big picture of a successful business. You budget to keep the business as healthy as possible to ensure that everyone can have a livelihood.

Other Expenses

We have covered the most important aspects of a profitable P&L, but there is a long way to go before you reach the net profit figure. Here are some expenses that are typical in your brewery profit and loss statement.

I've divided them into two areas: Controllable and Non-Controllable expenses. Controllable expenses are those you can control.

On the other hand, Non-Controllable are the expenses you can't control.

Controllable Expenses

Labor Taxes

Labor taxes are great because you don't have to "work" on it like you do all the others. That's because for every dollar you save on labor, you automatically save on payroll taxes too! Payroll taxes can run anywhere from 12% to 18% of your total payroll.

Repair & Maintenance

We covered this in the checklist section. The more proactive you are, the better. You should look at it as Repair and Preventative Maintenance. In your budget though, you should allow some money for the repairs that will come up. It is up to you to decide how much you want to put away each month to cover repairs but in our small operation I always budget in $500.

Pub Supplies

These are all the items you need to run your pub. Look at all of them from time to time and try to find less expensive alternatives to use. If you find a better and cheaper trash bag that costs .05 cents less and you go through 100 a month that's a savings of $60 a year. That would make a nice Christmas bonus for a dishwasher, and for no extra work. Other areas to save on are register paper, ink cartridges, and other office supplies. Stay out of office supply stores; you'll see all sorts of things you think you can't live without.

Brewery Supplies

I like to separate out brewery supplies from pub supplies. Brewery supplies cover things like brewing chemicals, keg caps, small fittings, dust masks, etc. It helps keep track of what it actually costs to make your beer.

Advertising

This will fluctuate depending on what time of year it is or what you want to push. Some advertising expenses will be every month, such as the yellow pages or the fees for your web site. Big companies allocate as much as 5% of gross receipts towards advertising. You may spend hardly anything and instead, use creativity to reach potential customers, such as Facebook and Twitter, or your own e-mail list.

Equipment Rental

This will include such things as an ice machine or dishwasher that can be rented. I usually would buy an ice machine because they don't cost very much and come with a good warranty. On the other hand I usually lease the dish machine because someone will come out and make sure it always runs well. You can decide what's good for you.

Replacement

This category is different from supplies because it is used for actually replacing items that are not just for one time use. This would include things like glassware, silverware, and china. If you notice replacement expenses as continually rising, you may want to look at a different type of pint glass that doesn't break as often. Or you may want to create a better system so that the dishwashers don't accidentally throw out silverware with the food scraps.

Utilities

Utilities can add up in no time. Many owners and managers walk into their business at 8:00 AM and immediately flick on every light in the place, even if they won't be open to the public until 11:00 AM. That's at least two and a half hours before they need to be on. If you multiply that two and a half hours times all the light bulbs and you would be surprised at the total hours used just in one day, let alone one year.

You will no doubt use some products that come in frozen. The health department states you need to defrost by running the product under a constant stream of water. Think about how much water that wastes! The other alternative is to use your checklists so that the day before the item needs to be used, it is taken from the freezer and placed in the refrigerator. This will eliminate all the time also that it takes to defrost underwater.

Brewers are geniuses at physics and process control. You will come up with all sorts of ways to save on your utility bill that will be good for your brewery, and good for the environment too.

For example there is a company called Freeaire (www.freeaire.com) that offers a system that lets in cold outside air in the winter into your walk-in cooler, and is regulated by an internal thermostat. So if you live in a climate that has winter you can essentially not run your compressors for six months out of the year. That is a huge payback in five years.

Music

Whether you pay for live entertainment or use recorded music, this is something you must have for your brewery. There are music services like satellite, cable or Muzak.

If you choose to just buy CD's or your iPod and play them, you are required to pay an ASCAP (American Society of Composers, Authors, and Publishers) fee for the royalties. The only way around the ASCAP fees is if you get the personal permission from the artists.

While it may not be that easy to get Eric Clapton to give you his permission to play his music, you could use local artists and those of the PutaMayo label, and then sells their CD's at your brewery.

Telephone

Telephone expenses can include bundling with your Internet service. You should have at least one phone line and a separate line for your credit card processing.

Non-Controllable Expenses

Every business has expenses that really cannot be controlled on a monthly basis. They have to be figured in if you are going to produce a preview P&L, or budget. Once you have all the numbers plugged in you can see if there will be anything left over that could be considered profit. Examples of these are to follow.

Business Loans

On an actual P&L, only interest is reported. For budget purposes however it is best to use the whole figure. On your P&L, you are not allowed to expense out the principal on a loan because it was never your money to begin with. You are just paying it back, so your only true expense is the interest you are paying. For your needs, you are still writing that check and it is money coming out of your cash flow. We need to account for it here.

Depreciation

The inverse is true for depreciation. Whereas with loan principal the money you spend to pay the loan back is not reported as an expense, this is something you can expense out according to the IRS. But, it is not actually money you are spending in the month. You spent it already in one large chunk and are spreading that expense over a longer period. Leave this figure out. We are only concerned with money that is actually being spent.

Rent, Insurance, Legal, Accounting & Credit Card Fees

I include credit card fees, because even though you can negotiate for lower fees, it is not really something you can control.

So there you have it, the whole P&L. With this information you create a P&L for the next month by plugging in all the numbers you know for a fact or can assume using historical information. If it shows a profit and you think it is fair, leave it alone. If it doesn't, or you think the profit isn't good enough, you can go back and adjust some of the numbers to bring the whole P&L into line with your expectations. This is your working budget.

When you are done, it will look something like this:

SALES $40,000.00
COST OF SALES @ 25% $10,000.00
GROSS PROFIT $30,000.00
LABOR @ 28%$11,200.00

NON-CONTROLLABLE EXPENSE

Labor Taxes $1,344.00

Supplies $900.00

Brewery Supplies $600.00

Replacement $250.00

Advertising $1,500.00

Equipment Rental $300.00

Repair & Maintenance $500.00

Music $35.00

Telephone $225.00

Utilities $1,200.00

CONTROLLABLE EXPENSE

Credit Card Fees $600.00

Insurance $800.00

Legal $0.00

Accounting $350.00

Rent $1,500.00

Bank Loan $4,000.00

TOTAL EXPENSES $14,104.00

NET PROFIT $4,696.0

Tracking Sales With Your Score Board

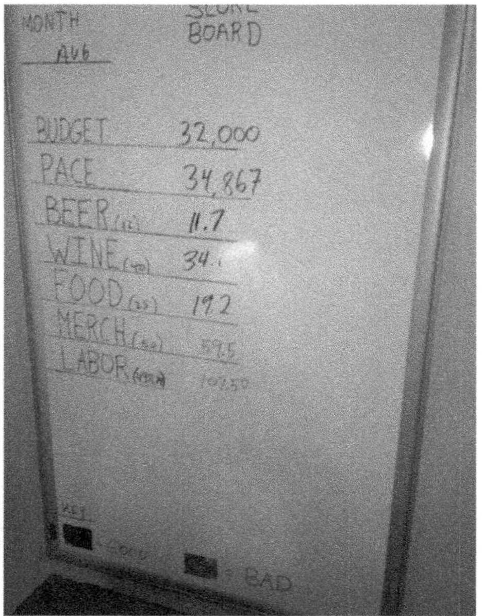

Our Messy But Effective Scoreboard

Can you imagine playing baseball and not keeping score? What would be the fun in that? Well that, however, is usually how we go about running a business. We play each daily inning not knowing if we are winning or losing the game.

To make things more interesting in our day-to-day running of the brewery, we want to create a scoreboard that will tell us on a daily basis the score. It will also indicate whether we are making a profit. Here we'll rely on the 80/20 principal again and just concentrate on the big three-Sales, Cost of Sales, and Labor. If we are hitting our targets in these areas, then we should be 80% of the way towards profitability.

How to Create Your Own Score Board

1. Buy one of those big dry erase boards and put this up in your office prominently where you will see it every day.
2. At the top you will write the *Month* in, and the *Current Date.*
3. You will write your *Sales* budget figure, and *Sales Pace* (I'll explain in a minute).
4. Write the *Cost of Sales* percentages that you calculated from your most recent inventory.
5. At the bottom of the board you will write *Labor Bank.*

Now, here is how we arrive at these numbers.

Sales Pace

Remember we went over this when we looked at how to do the daily books. On that sheet you recorded your sales pace. The sales pace is the pace the business is on if it continues to run at the current sales volume. For example, if five days into the month you have done $5,000 in sales, you can assume you might do $30,000 in sales for the month.

In other words, if you averaged $1,000 a day for the first five days, that "might" translate into a continuing trend of $1,000 a day for the rest of the month. Of course, that is not how real life is. You also have to consider how many weekends there are in the month, special holidays, etc. But you would be surprised at how close you will come by figuring it this way.

The Formula: Take the current total sales, divided by how many days so far in the month, multiplied by the total number of business days in the month. Don't forget that tax collected is not counted as sales.

Let's say on the 17th of the month you see that you have done

$42,387.22 in sales. Remember, on our daily sales report, it will show this figure. Divide this number by 17 (the 17 full days of prior sales), which equal $2,493.36. This is your daily average. Next, multiply this number by the total number of business days in the month, which in this case is 31, and your projected sales for the month is $77,294.16.

Now, at the beginning of the month you had budgeted for $75,000 in sales based on last year's sales of $72,750 and you have been averaging 3% growth from the prior year. So here you now have two figures, one is your budget of $75,000.00, the other is the sales pace you are on as of the current date, which is $77,294.16. Pretty good so far.

Cost of Sales

This is one thing you probably can't check every day. Remember that to figure your cost of sales, you have to do inventories. If your inventories are large as they are in a grocery store, it might be a once a year thing. In a small brewery, it can be done once a month or maybe even once a week. Once a month is adequate and more can keep you more finely tuned in to the pulse of your business.

In review, to obtain the cost of sales you take the beginning inventory, plus purchases (any new inventory you bought), minus an ending inventory. This will equal the cost of sales in dollars. This is then divided by the corresponding sales for the inventory period, which will yield your cost as a percentage. It is this important percentage that you write down on your scoreboard with the date of the last time you calculated it.

I also like to write down what my target percentage is. For example if your beer target was 12%, you would write that down next to "Beer" then have a line for what your actual current percent was, say 11.2%.

Labor

Labor is figured in the same way we figured sales. First, you come up with your budgeted labor for the month. You can do this a couple of different ways as we discussed earlier. Then you can look at what you average per month and try to beat this figure. Third, you can make up an ideal schedule and multiply it by wages to see what it comes out to. As I mentioned earlier, I like to do it this way because it is more realistic.

Calculating Daily Labor Cost

After you have figured out what your monthly labor budget is, divide that figure by the number of days you are going to be open during the month. This will give you your daily labor budget. You can compare this figure against what you actually spent.

To calculate your daily labor, just write down on a piece of paper the employee hours every day and multiply it by their wage. This will give you the total money spent. Most likely your register system will spit out a daily report of what you spent, if your employees are clocking in and out on the register. You can also make up a work sheet to do this. In addition, if you have employees that are on salary, take that total and divide it by the number of days per month. This daily total is then added to your other total wages for a grand total.

Labor Bank

Here's how it works. Let's say you figure you can spend $500 a day per your budget. This includes you. The first day you spend $499. This means you have $1 left over. This is the number you write down in your labor bank. It's like a bank account. You have daily deposits and daily withdrawals. It is real money in real time. The next day you spend

$550 and you update your labor bank to show <$49>. That's your positive $1 minus your negative $50.

With this information, you become determined. The next day you let some people off 15 minutes early because it was slow, and they were more than happy to go. This day you spent $460. You tabulate your labor bank (because it is on your daily checklist to do so) and now you are only <$9>. Much better. You tell yourself that the next day you will save even more.

As you go through the month you will find that it is easy to save when the numbers are right in front of you. This is real money. If you come to the end of the month, and you have a positive balance in your labor bank, you will have extra cash. Perhaps you have some extra cleaning you can pay some employees to do, or whatever else you decide to do with it.

In putting it all together, you walk in to your brewery on a Tuesday having had Sunday and Monday off. You check your scoreboard and see the Sales Budget of $70,000 and a Sales Pace of $71, 482.32. Cost of Sales are all up to date and running within the margins you want. The Labor Bank shows <$23.00>. Not too bad. The managers aren't as good as you in getting people off the clock, but the other numbers look great! This week you'll work on the labor and bring it up for discussion at the next manager meeting.

Sample Score Board

AS OF ____/____/____

SALES BUDGET $40,000
SALES PACE $41,200

COST OF SALES

FOOD (30%) 27.48%
BEVERAGES (12%) 10.58%
MERCHANDISE (50%) 45.45%
BEER (12%) 11.2%

LABOR BANK < $12.85>

There you have it. You know what the score is. You know if your brewery is winning or losing without having to wait for the end of the month and into the next one for the accountant to produce a P&L for you. You have your finger on the pulse of your business in real time. You are running it well, thanks to your checklists.

Things look rosy, but how do you keep it this way day in and day out? Will everyone continue to do his or her checklists? Will employees really be trained according to your systems? Will the managers keep up with the scoreboard on a daily basis like you would? This is where we bring in the practice of auditing.

Audits

One of the hardest things to do personally and in business is to be consistent. We promise ourselves all sorts of things, from new exercise programs or reading one book per week, to vowing to eat healthier. And we do it for a couple of weeks, or until something interrupts our new routine before it has a chance to become habit. Then the whole thing falls by the wayside. What we need is someone who will call us on it, to hold us accountable. It's a pretty tall order in business though when you are the boss. You are not held accountable to anyone, and you need to be. Especially, if you want all of this hard work to bear fruit!

I have found that the best way to do this is with an audit system. This is a way to check and make sure that everything within your system is being done. You will do the auditing, or, each manager will audit his or her own area or each other's. In addition, you will have someone from outside your brewery audit as well. They will audit the auditors. This will keep the auditors honest. Sound confusing? Here's how it works.

The Internal Audit

An internal audit is basically a checklist of things that should be done on an ongoing basis. With this audit, you will see if all your systems are working and that your managers and staff are doing their jobs.

Determine How the Brewery Should Look

First, assign an area of your brewery to a manager, or yourself if you are the only one managing and make a list of how that area should look. Include everything you can think of. Remember the perfect employee? Include items like the cleanliness of the light fixtures, the walls and floors. Are the bathrooms clean and in good repair, is the artwork hanging straight?

Also to be checked would be all the areas within the pub to see that the employees are doing their side-work. Include checking basic things like windows for cleanliness, dust bunnies in the vents, or trash outside the front door.

Financial Information

In addition to these checklist items, you should also include financial information that your scoreboard reflects: Sales, Cost of Sales, and Labor. Every manager has a hand in this. If the Cost of Sales is high, it is important to find out the cause and make adjustments as soon as possible. If your sales are just under what was predicted in your budget, then it is every manager's responsibility to do whatever they can to increase sales. The financial items on the audit sheets are the same for every manager.

Weekly Audits

Audits are to be done once a week and turned in at the weekly manager's meeting. Auditing needs to happen at some point during the seven days. When it is done depends on your managers' available time. It's not a big deal and may only take five minutes depending on how involved it is.

No one needs to look over their shoulders while they do this. It is up to the manager to be honest in what they see. If something is not getting done in their area as often as needed, they can change an employee's checklist. They want to be sure the job gets done well enough to reflect in the audit. This area is totally up to them. They can manage it as they see fit as long as it holds up to the standards set forth in the internal audit. But, just to make it more fun and be able to relate the audit to bonuses, it needs to be scored.

Sample Internal Audit Sheet

Dining Room		*Financial*	
2	Floors Clean	10	*Score Board Up To Date*
2	Baseboards Clean	10	Food Cost 22%
2	Walls Clean	10	Beer Cost 12%
2	Table Bases Clean	10	Beverage Cost 28%
2	Chairs Clean	4	Merchandise Cost 55%
2	Lights Dusted	4	Employee Files Up To Date
2	All Light bulbs Working	4	Office Clean
2	Ceiling Clean	4	All Paper Work Filed
2	Vents Clean		
2	Pictures Hung Straight		
2	Windows Clean		
Restrooms		2	Floors Clean
2	Baseboards Clean	2	Walls Clean
2	Ceiling Clean	2	Toilets Clean
2	Sink Clean	2	Lights Dusted
2	Sink Fixture Clean	2	All Light Bulbs Working
2	Vents Clean	2	Door Clean

SCORE______________________ DATE__________________________
MANAGER______________________

Scoring The Audit

Stocking widgets on a shelf is work. Stocking widgets on a shelf, but doing it faster than the guy next to you is fun! Work can become a game, if you know the rules.

There is an excellent book I recommend called "The Game Of Work" by Charles A. Coonradt. He wonders why people would complain about how physically hard their work is, and then go play football on the weekend and get totally beat up! The answer is simple; one is a game and the other isn't.

Wouldn't it be an improvement if work could turn into a game?

That's the idea in scoring audits. You can do this with your audits or anything else in your brewery, but first there are a few guidelines you must follow to create a good game.

1. Keep score
2. Post the scores
3. Put the players in charge of the scores
4. Make sure everyone knows the rules, and don't change them
5. List the rewards and penalties and stick to them

How to Score the Audit

When we score our audits we are creating part of this game. An easy way to score the audit sheet is to assign a number next to an item to be audited. I like to make things add up to 100. This is easy to understand and gives you lots of opportunities to weigh the audit. For example, you might have the "lights dusted" as counting for two points while having the "sales budget met" worth 15.

Start by assigning a number of points next to each audit item that is to be checked. The key is that the total points add up to 100. It is up to you how many points you assign to each item. It depends on what you think is important. However, it is best to emphasize the most important three items- Sales, Cost of Sales, and Labor.

Once you have assigned numbers to your categories, you need to think of a scoring system. Here is one that works. 90 to 100 equals 100%, 80 to 89 equals 90%, 70 to 79 equal 80%. If you are having them done once a week, you take the average of the scores for the month and that is the score you post and the score you might use to help calculate bonuses.

My experience is that it is difficult to get 100% on the audit. If the score is 90 or above, it means that the system is working. If the score is an 85 that equals a 90% because it is not bad, but needs improving. If someone is scoring below a 70, that means they are not doing their job.

No matter how much you trust your people to be doing their audits accurately, you need a system to check up on them. This is where an external audit comes in.

The External Audit

Even the best plans have holes in them. There may be a time when you or the managers just don't feel like following the systems or doing your internal audit sincerely. It might be there just isn't enough time or something else more important comes up. These are the times that can cause the whole system to break down.

One of the best ways to insure that the audits are done accurately and turned in when they are supposed to is to instigate an external audit. This audit will be done to basically verify that the other audits are correct and therefore the system is working.

The external audit is like the internal audits, but combined into one. It should have everything that is on the individual audits but may include some additional things you would like to have verified. Of particular importance, other than making sure all the checklists have been followed, is to be sure that the books are done correctly.

Things to Check

- Daily sales reports agree with the register tape
- Daily sales reports agree with the deposit slips from the bank
- Daily sales reports are added accurately
- Scoreboard is up to date and correct
- Invoices are divided into their proper expense categories and filed to be paid

- Checklists are being used
- Office is clean and organized
- Employee folders are complete and accurate

To score this audit, you may need more than one page. One way you can do it is to have each page add up to 100 and give each item a score, like you did in the internal audit. Here they would be weighted as well. So Office Clean might be worth 4 points, while the Scoreboard up to date might be worth 15 points. To give an overall score, calculate the average of all the pages. This becomes the score for the external audit.

Who Does the External Audit?

As the owner, you may want to do the external audit. Or, you can bring someone in from the outside and train him or her on the system to do it. The external audit will need to be done once a month, and can be anytime during that month. This is an important factor in the external audit. Because it is a surprise visit, you and the managers need to be always on top of the system in order to do well on the external audit score. This is important because we can use the external audit score to calculate bonuses!

Too Complicated?

If you would like to simplify this whole scenario, get rid of the internal audit and just have an external audit done once per month. It should still be complete and unannounced. It will be your report card on how well you are following your own systems. It is also an excellent way to help calculate bonuses for your key people.

The Bonus System

Remember that we have created a game with our audits. Now it is time to tell the managers what they get if they win. Many bonus systems are purely subjective. If the business makes money, the owner gives out an amount that he or she feels they can afford, or, something extra at Christmas. This works, as it truly is a bonus. The manager or employee doesn't really expect it. The bonus is just something extra.

A bonus system gets your key people involved in the mechanics of your brewery. If what they do impacts your business, it only makes sense to let them in on how it makes money and to reward them accordingly. It develops a sense of ownership in the manager or brewer towards the brewery. No one runs a business as well as someone who owns it. By distributing bonuses to key employees, you are making them players in the game.

Active participants need to know the score, and they also need to know that if they win or lose, WHAT they win or lose. Money speaks the loudest. They can consistently win $200 per month (or whatever you feel is appropriate), or not get that money, if the business is losing.

You can really make up any kind of game you want. What I offer here is just one way to make a bonus system. You can use it, change it, or discard it. Just stick to the important aspects that we mentioned earlier:

1. The rules are clearly known.
2. The scores are posted
3. The game is self-regulated.
4. The participants can calculate what the bonus will be based on the above.

Bonus Calculations

Many small businesses don't have a system for figuring out bonuses. Some give money to key people when they feel the business is profiting and they want to show their gratitude. As I said before, it may be motivated by some special event like the holidays, or a manager going on vacation. These are fine times to do this, but they hardly fit into the rules of a good game.

With a bonus system, you want to satisfy that most basic need of "what's in it for me". It really is important for your key people to see that they will somehow benefit from their efforts to run the brewery well. Also, a bonus is a way for you, the owner to say to your key people that you know they are doing a good job. We all long for some sort of recognition for a job well done.

There are many ways to calculate a bonus. It could be a straight percent of sales or net profit for example. However, the problem with doing it this way is that you can have good sales and not make a profit. Or you can show a net profit that isn't a true picture of profitability. You may have some expenses that only relate to the owner and a manager has no control over them. So how do you figure out a fair way? I like to make it based on facets of the business your manager can actually control. The way I calculate this is to take sales, minus cost of sales, minus labor, minus controllable expenses, equals an amount that I take a percentage of.

Sales – Cost of Sales – Labor – Controllable Expenses

= Bonus Fund

The bonus fund is the money left over after this calculation. The manager gets a percentage of this. For example a General Manager might get 2.5%, while a shift manager may get 1%. You decide the rules of the game.

Remember that controllable expenses are items like supplies, utilities, repairs, advertising, replacement, etc. You will come up with a list that fits your brewery.

What is emphasized with managers and yourself is to always apply your effort from the top down. Work on sales first, then cost of sales, and labor before you start creating a program to change light bulbs to compact fluorescent to save on electricity. Remember the 80/20 principal. Spending that extra hour of effort on sales will go a lot further than spending it on utilities!

Once you have calculated your bonus fund, you can assign a bonus percentage to each employee. For example, the assistant manager could get 2% of that fund. A shift manager might get 1.5%. You can use the percent figure in raises also. Instead of a raise in salary, you can raise them from 1.5% bonus to 2% bonus. That way it is based on their good work. It allows a lot of flexibility in compensation.

Once a manager knows the formula, it becomes real. When someone can actually calculate it themselves based on real numbers, they know the score and can play to win!

How the Audit Effects Bonuses

It is one thing to show a profit, but what good is it if it comes at the expense of customer service, lack of repairs, or other necessary expenses? You audit to make sure everything is running according to your system. You need to give the audit some teeth and bring it into the game. You do this by having it affect the bonuses.

Audit Scores & Bonuses

Use this score as a multiplier against the bonus fund. This can be customized in a number of different ways to suit your special needs in your brewery. If the audit is 90 or above, that would count as a 100, so you would multiply it against the bonus fund and they would get 100% of what that fund is. But if the manager's score was an 87, and you consider any score of 80 to 89 as a 90%, then multiply their bonus fund by 90%.

Your management can actually see how much money they didn't receive because of the audit. You may consider anything below a 70 as a "bonus out of bounds" which would mean that their audit was so poor they receive no bonus. Or, you might say that a 95 or higher on the external audit counts for a 110% of the bonus. You see it is up to you.

Chapter 14

THE OYSTER: CREATING AN ATMOSPHERE

An oyster is your retail environment. Why an "oyster" you ask? Because an oyster is its own private world protected by a shell from the outside. It is also a living thing, changing to suit the environment. Alive. The oyster in a retail setting is the environment you create for your customers. Another way to think of it is as if you are putting on a play and creating a stage setting that sets the mood for your customers. You are creating an environment that is friendly, comfortable, and inviting folks to stay a while.

Every business has an oyster, especially a brewery. Some by virtue of their environment and architecture, some out of ignorance of the owners, and some deliberate. Take what you learn from this step and start looking around at different restaurants and bars and you will see what I mean.

Take for example a cafe in a small town in Italy. Weathered walls, clean but old and chipped floor tiles, walls covered in old photographs, open bottles of mineral water on tables with fresh flowers and clean linen table clothes. Outside the fragrance of olive trees, and the sun beaming through the imperfect panes of old glass windows. This oyster was created over time; with the help of geography and culture; it is unique. You could ask how can they help it when they have so much inherent is this setting? I say you create your oyster. In Italy you are just as likely to find a business with no art, white walls, fluorescent lights humming, chipped cheap furniture and slovenly employees.

In America you can go into a Pottery Barn store and find furniture displayed in settings right out of Architectural Digest. With just the right lighting, contemporary music, and props like old books, and art to give the feeling of what home could be like if you only had that type of furniture. In other words as soon as you walk into a Pottery Barn you walk into their world. In effect is a fantasy world; a fantasy that you would like to be a part of. On the other hand, you could walk into a real estate office with gray carpet, white walls, fluorescent lights, no art on the walls, agents dressed any way they want, and no music, just a hushed sound of people typing or talking on the phone. Sounds familiar doesn't it?

What if you walked into a real estate office and it looked like Pottery Barn? Light wood floors with beautiful rugs, light spreading warmth from tasteful lamps and overhead track lights spotting paintings and sculpture, Dave Brubeck playing from a quality sound system in the background, and furniture that is comfortable and attractive. The staff wearing a tasteful shirt with the company's logo embroidered on the pocket. You are about to shell out the most money you will ever spend in your life. Wouldn't you feel better about it in this place than the cold office first described?

In a brewery, the oyster is everything! My wife Sandy and I were in Scotland and on the first night we were looking for a place to eat in small town up in the Highlands. The weather was wet, and cool. Night was coming on early since Scotland is no far north. We found a pub. As we walked in the door the temperature was warm and inviting. There was some nice jazz playing and the bartender greeted us right away. After looking through the menu I picked a steak and ale pie and a best bitter on cask from the local brewery. The food was rich and savory and the bitter was like silk. I had tears in my eyes the experience was so good. You can create just as fulfilling an experience here by following some simple rules.

There are five parts that make up the oyster.

1. Lighting
2. Music
3. Temperature
4. Cleanliness
5. Stage Setting.

Each one is very important and connected to the others. Also, each aspect is constantly changing. To manage the oyster is not that difficult once you get the hang of it. Let's look at each one separately.

LIGHTING

I can't say enough about lighting. In so many businesses it is taken for granted. With just a little imagination, it can be the most positive way you have to present your brewery to customers.

There are no steadfast rules to lighting because there are so many types of businesses. Some businesses need a lot of lighting set on the highest setting. Other businesses like restaurants, coffee houses and of course brewpubs, need lighting that is more subtle and adjustable.

Take for example Safeway. Many of their stores used to have an institutional feeling about them. They had bright fluorescent lights that made it easy to see their products. The problem was that with that type of lighting made everything and everyone in the store look cold and gray. In the past few years many have re-modeled and followed the example of lighting in the very popular Whole Foods chain. They also use fluorescent lights, but only as a fill in. The majority of the lights are pendants with regular light bulbs. The lights look like the old warehouse type but they give off a warmer glow which not only makes the products look more appealing (like you would see them in your home) but also makes the people shopping look better. Remember fluorescent lights not only make the products gray, it doesn't help the skin color either. Here are some points we can learn from these markets.

Avoid sole use of fluorescents lights.
Put lights on a dimmer switch.
Be creative in choosing light fixtures.

A brewery doesn't need fluorescent lights, except perhaps in the back kitchen, out of the public view, or if you are packaging, you may need them on the bottling line. Pick lights that match the type of stage setting you intend. You might just use track lighting, recessed lights, pendant lights, or a combination of all three. The important thing is to have the lights on a dimmer switch, which is an on/off switch and adjustable. This way you can adjust the lights according to the outside natural light.

The general rule that I find works best is that when the sun is at the brightest, you keep the lights on their highest to balance out the sun light. But, as the sun goes down, so do the lights, softening the effect. If the lights are not bright enough during the day to balance the sunlight, then the space feels too dark. If the lights are too bright when the sun goes down, it makes the space feel too cold and empty. However, if the light is too dark inside when the sun goes down, then it is hard to see. You can mark your dimmers for the day and night shifts, but remember there is the in between time when you need to adjust them in small increments. Also remember when adjusting your lights to do it slowly. Slowly enough so the adjustment is imperceptible to the customer.

Lighting can also be used as one of the main design elements in your space. One thing that is cost effective is to scrimp on some things in your space and go all out on lighting. It will indicate to your customers that you spent a lot because you care about the atmosphere. People feel cared for in a space that is inviting.

Interesting light fixtures can say a lot about your brewery too. Using lights as a design element can make the retail space more fun and creative. If you don't see the type of lights you want, you can always invent your own using your imagination and whatever materials you can scrounge up. These days anything goes for light fixtures. Make them fun, make them interesting, but most of all make lighting inviting.

Making good use of natural light enhances the Oyster as well. You can use shades creatively or the placement of the seating in the windows. The added bonus of seating in the windows is that your brewery always looks full because people passing by always see people inside.

MUSIC

Music is one of my favorite subjects within the oyster theme. It can add so much to the brewpub environment without costing very much. Everyone is used to music in shopping malls, restaurants and elevators. But the vast majority of businesses do not use this proven tool to their full advantage. I don't know if it is due to ignorance or perhaps the business owner just doesn't think about it. But, to create a great oyster, attention to music is a must!

There are two key factors that have to do with having music in your business. They are the type of music and the volume of the music playing.

The type of music depends on many factors. One factor is the type of brewery you have. Colorado Boy has some inspiration from those small town Scottish breweries I visited, but still has roots in Colorado. Our music is a mix that is contemporary and Celtic, with a little jazz thrown in. You may want more Reggae or Ska, or perhaps Patsy Cline. Play around with it and you will figure out what is right for you. Base your choices on creating a desired atmosphere and not so much on your personal taste or that of your employees.

As for the volume of the music, this depends on the sound level of your brewery. A good starting point would be to adjust the level to your normal speaking level. If it is early and there are only a few customers in, you might want the music a little higher, to help fill in the silent gaps, making the pub feel less vacant. However, if the brewery is jamming, you might not want to have any music at all, or at least not as loud. When there is too much activity the extra music just makes the whole scene feel out of control.

As with lighting, you rarely can set the volume level and just leave it. Depending on how the music is mixed, some songs just seem louder than others. Or there may be an intense guitar or horn solo. Things that just don't fit into the current flow of the business. Experiment with the volume. Turn the volume all the way down and watch your customers. You can actually feel the discomfort level. People start speaking more quietly so they can't be overheard. By playing with the volume control you will find the right level for your brewery, the time of day and the number of customers in the pub.

TEMPERTATURE

Correct temperature equals comfort. It's that simple. The temperature inside your brewery fluctuates according to the outside temperature, and how many people are in the seating area. Temperature has a psychological impact on your customers. For example, it may be snowing outside. Rather than a comfortable 70 degrees, you boost the thermostat to 75. The customer comes in from the snow to a blast of warm air and the sounds of a busy pub, welcoming them into the comfort of your brewery. Or, if it is sweltering outside and you have a good air conditioner, the customer gets that blast of cool air and you can actually see the relaxation in their face and body.

In business we sometimes tend to forget about the temperature of our establishments unless the heating or cooling unit is broken. We also are not good indicators of the temperature because we are usually running around doing things which makes us feel a little warmer than a customer just coming in the door. One good thing we can do is to watch our customers' body language. If a customer feels cold in your brewery, you can tell by the way they cross their arms, or put their hands in their pockets, or keep their jackets on. An all too common thing is the air conditioner on too high and the room too cold. This is because the staff is running around and they are hot. Meanwhile the poor customers are freezing. It's not a very enticing environment for drinking a cold pint.

CLEANLINESS

So why is cleanliness so important, I mean aside from the obvious? When a customer walks into your brewery and everything is clean and neat, there is a sense of order about the place. Think of how you feel in your own home. If there are dirty dishes in the sink, the trashcan in the bathroom is over flowing, the bed not made and clothes on the floor, you feel a little out of control. It's upsetting. You feel better when you take the time to do the dishes, empty the garbage, make the bed, hang up the clothes, heck, even vacuum and do laundry. Now you feel like you're really on top of it. This is a good feeling you can't deny it. You may even vow to always be this way.

Walk into a small retail shop and the service counter is cluttered with paperwork, the counter-persons lunch, and old coffee stains. It's not a pleasant feeling. However the same store that has a clean counter looks like it's ready for business, instead of trying to "catch up". It just puts you at ease. The following are some areas of particular importance for your brewery.

The Parking Lot

Get rid of cigarette butts, and general trash. Pull weeds and if you can, plant flowers. This is the first area your customer sees and it will say a lot about your brewery. It's not a big deal to keep it clean. Remember, you must add it to a checklist.

The Front Door Area

This includes clean glass, door surfaces, and the floor on the outside and inside of the door. Remember to keep the handles to the door clean. You don't know what sticky substance was on the little kids' hands when they used it last.

The Restrooms

This is a biggie. Clean restrooms say a lot about your businesses' organizational ability. It always gripes me to see large national chains have these really polished retail areas and trashed bathrooms. If I see a dirty and unsanitary bathroom in a restaurant, I also can't help but wonder how clean they keep the kitchen! Once a restroom is really clean, it only takes a couple of minutes a day to keep it that way. And then add a few small touches like flowers, or a side table where a woman can place her purse while using the restroom and you've made a lot of customers relaxed and happy.

Floors and Walls

Put these on a regular maintenance schedule. Floors if they are the high polished kind, need to stay that way. Carpets need to be cleaned on a regular basis to avoid dark paths. Tile floors collect dirt in the grout seems. Walls suffer from stains and chips taken out while moving things around. Touch up the paint often and repaint when needed. Once again, these items should be on a checklist for maintenance and an audit sheet.

Light Fixtures

These are natural collectors of dust and spider webs. Look up when doing your audits to see these. It should be on a checklist to dust them at least once a week depending on the kind of brewery you have.

Displays

They should be spotless. After all they are displays - get it? You don't want to display dirt! This means not only having the glass clean, but also everything neatly organized.

The cleanliness of your brewery is a direct result of successful implementation of your checklist and audit systems. What you are giving your customers is sense of order in a crazy world that they must deal with once they leave your place. Don't give them more of the same.

STAGE SETTING

So what the heck is your brewery all about anyway? Stage setting is the "touchy feely" part of the oyster. It's what you are trying to convey to your customers about you. A small example would be our personal stage settings; our homes, our clothes, and the cars we drive. They all are picked out because it portrays to the rest of the world what we believe we are. I may drive a sports car because I want people to think I'm exciting. I may wear the latest fashions so I will look cool. It's the same in our brewery.

Look at Eddie Bauer. They sell clothes. So what's with the old books and lamps and canoes? It is because they are selling a lifestyle. Kind of that Ernest Hemmingway thing! It goes further too. Nice rich wood interior, slow moving ceiling fans (Casa Blanca), easy lighting, with appropriate music. It's a whole atmosphere.

So again, what the heck is your brewery going to be? It can be a simple counter and chairs with some beer taps, or so much more. Look at other business possibilities. You could own a regular gas station, or a throwback to the gas stations of the past where service and professionalism ruled the road. You can have a regular pet store or one that is a slice of a South American Jungle! Here are some other examples to give you a feel for what I mean:

Hair salon as a cool pool hall that also cuts hair
Home decorating center as a furnished home
Real estate office as a rustic, cozy cabin
French restaurant seeming to be in a French village
Music shop in a sound studio
A café in a setting that shows old time movies
Painting supply store or art gallery that sells house paint.
You get the idea!

First decide what you want to say about your brewery. Not just what you want to sell. People make purchases on feelings, not always what they need. What kind of feeling are you trying to get across to your customer?

Once you know, then you use the tools previously mentioned to achieve it with the addition of props. Props can be anything. Eddie Bauer uses canoes. McDonalds uses a playground. Blockbuster uses many TV's showing featured movies. If I had a pet shop I'd use a lot of big fake plants and an old jeep in the middle of the store with headlights that worked and a humidifier hooked up to the exhaust. We have a local boarding kennel designed to make pet owners feel as if they are dropping their pet off for camp. This can be the fun part of creating your business oyster!

Once you know what your brewery is about, then your imagination can really take off. The oyster is about what your business says to the customer. Just being aware that you need an oyster puts you ahead of most competition. Give it a try. This is one thing that will keep customers coming back.

Chapter 15

THE GREEN BREWERY

Instituting green practices in your brewery of course is the right thing to do and the type of customers that are attracted to craft beer appreciate that you take care of our natural resources as well, so it's good PR. But the bottom line is that it costs money NOT to be green.

Being green is being efficient. A brewery is a factory after all. Energy efficiency squandered is money wasted. So here are a few ideas to juice up your imagination on things you can do in your now completed brewery that will save you money and leave you feeling good about it.

Don't Waste The Grain

Every brewer gives or charges a nominal fee for the spent grain left over from the brewing process. While it is not suitable for horses; cows, pigs and chickens love it! We give ours to a local ranch for their cows, and another farm to feed their chickens. We in turn get the fresh eggs that we use on our pizzas.

Don't Waste Water

A lot of water gets used in cleaning, because cleaning is mostly what we do in breweries. However, even more water is used in the heat exchange process. One simple thing to do that will not cost you any money is to recapture that heat exchange water in your mash tun.

I find that I have enough time after all the wort is transferred to the kettle to completely clean out the mash tun before the kettle comes to a boil. Then, when I am transferring the wort through the heat exchanger at the end of the day, I send the now hot water coming out of the heat exchanger to the mash tun. If you do this, make sure you use a good hose and not a garden hose to feed cold water to the heat exchanger. A garden hose will make the water taste like a rubber garden hose.

When you are done with the transfer you should have 150 to 200 gallons of fairly hot water. Ours runs about 150 degrees out of the heat exchanger. This can be used for cleaning at the end of the day, or for your next brew. You end up saving all those BTU's and water as well.

Trash Bags

Here is a simple one; what to do with all those grain bags? We save them and use them as our kitchen trash bags. They are very sturdy and don't leak. They may be a little funky in size compared to the plastic bags but we go through about two per night saving the landfill from about 700 extra trash bags per year. Each trash bag costs about .22 cents each, so we are also saving about $154 per year. If you were to net 10% you would have to do an extra $1,540 in sales to make that kind of money. That's a lot of pints!

Solar Hot Water

Heating your water from the sun is more expensive. We did it anyway. We have 30 solar tubes on our roof and 200 gallons of solar heated water storage. The sun heats the water, which then goes through a hot water on demand system heating only what we need. Without a conventional hot water heater, our gas only heats water as we need it, rather than keeping a tank of hot water available at all times. Our monthly gas bill runs about $60 to $70, and that figure covers all our hot water needs; the restaurant and brewpub, the gas kettle, and gas forced air heat. Not bad! And it is something we are proud of. And, it has gotten us good press.

Cooling

If your brewery is in a climate that has a cold winter, it makes good sense to use the cold air that nature provides. There is a company called Free Air (freeair.com), which has developed a system that brings in the cold outside air to run your coolers instead of using expensive compressors. It is a little pricey up front but provides a payback in as little as two years. If you were a microbrewer and had a large walk-in cooler, this would be a good way to go. Not only would you be saving on electricity half the year, but, your compressors would last twice as long. Your customers would be impressed too.

Altruism aside, it doesn't hurt to let your customers know that you follow green business practices. Let them know by informing them through your Facebook page, or explanations on your menus or tables tents. Devote a page on your web site to this and allow feedback and ideas from your customers. You could award free beer for the best idea of the month.

Chapter 16

MAKING MONEY

Sometimes we get lost in the adventure of building a brewery and forget that on top of the perks of being our own boss, we can also make money in our venture. However, like all things, success doesn't just happen. You have to create it.

Even when you are making a good monthly net profit, you need a system for managing that profit. Profits can leak out during the course of a year. It is possible to end up with nothing to show for your labor come New Year's Eve. In order to build wealth, you need to use the same practices that make individuals wealthy, and simply apply them to your brewery. You need to know how to squeeze all the value out of each and every dollar, through budgeting, saving, and investing.

Through these practices, you can build up a substantial amount of money, without having a huge business. That is because time goes by. I repeat. Time goes by. Five or ten years can quickly slip away. If you have a plan to carry you through those years, you will be amply rewarded. The two magic ingredients of time and compound interest can be your incredibly valuable allies.

Compound Interest & Debt

I like to think of compound interest as a steep hill. People are either on one side of this hill or the other. To the left, is compound interest that must be paid BY an individual. To the right, is compound interest that is paid TO an individual. Another way to look at it is that society is divided into two types of people. One half pays interest, and the other half receives it.

When you first start out in business, you accumulate a lot of debt. Your $200,000 loan may seem like a deal at 9% for 7 years (if you can get 7 year financing), but is it really? Let's look at it more closely. By the time you pay off your $200,000, you will have paid $70,295.16 in interest! That works out to 35.14%. When you are paying it off you are looking up from the bottom of a steep slope towards the debt-free top. Of the monthly payment, most of it is interest-hence the steepness. Looking at the first year on that note, you have paid $21,485.74 in principal (actual borrowed money paid back), and $17, 127.98 in interest. That is a lot of interest compared to principal. By the end of the note, the ratio begins to level off. That last year you pay $36,795.48 in principal, and $1,818.30 in interest. At the top of the hill you are debt-free, you owe no interest and receive no interest.

For businesses, you can't really move to the other side of the hill, because the government doesn't like businesses to retain profits. You cannot leave the money in the company to earn compounding interest. It needs to be spent on capital improvements, dispersed as compensation and therefore triggering taxes. This is where you need a good accountant who can show you ways to minimize taxes while increasing compensation. With compensation you can use the money to move you yourself to the good side of the interest hill.

Paying Off Debt

Many accountants do not like businesses to pay off debt too quickly because this creates phantom income. This is due to the fact that you can only expense interest, not principal. Let me explain. You never really owned the principal. It wasn't your money; you borrowed it. When you write that loan payment check every month, the principal you pay back wasn't yours in the first place so it is not considered a legitimate expense. Only the interest that you pay on that payment is considered your money, and therefore you are allowed to expense that portion of the payment.

So going back to the example above, you paid $21,485.74 in principal your first year, and $17,127.98 in interest. The interest goes on your profit and loss statement as an expense, so where does the principal go? Down to the bottom line as profit! Profit that you gave back to the lender and that you are taxed on even though you don't actually have the cash anymore. That is why it is called phantom income. A good accountant can help you deal with this issue, and hopefully still pay the loan off earlier. Let me show you why this is a good idea.

If you pay off your loan in seven years, you will pay $3,217.80 in payments over that loan period, totaling $70,296.30 in interest. But if you can swing an extra $1,000 per month, you can pay the loan off in five years and save $21,197.42. That is significant. It also makes the interest hill a little smaller. The key is to generate cash to do this, and to do this you have to learn the value of money.

Here is how I look at the value of money as it relates to your brewery. It is also a good math lesson to teach your employees. First of all, let's assume that you are netting 8% profit before taxes – not a bad net profit. Every time you spend money on expense items, that is money that normally would go straight to the bottom line in the form of net profit, had you not spent it.

EXAMPLE 1

Suppose you bought a box of mechanical pencils for $9.95 at the office supply store. How much in the way of sales do you need in order to produce enough profit to pay for those pencils? The easiest way to figure it out is to divide the purchase by your net profit percentage, which is .08.

You need to sell an extra $124.37 in beer to produce enough profit to cover your purchase. A box of number 2 pencils costs about $1.75 or equals $21.87 in sales. An added bonus is no one will be tempted to steal a number 2 pencil. However, they might if it was a nice mechanical pencil, so the pencils will probably last longer.

You see every time you spend a dollar there is a corresponding sale that needs to take place to pay for the purchase.

EXAMPLE 2

By cleaning the refrigerator compressor every week, it extends the life of the unit. A compressor costs $500, so if you didn't clean it regularly and keep it in good working order, the associated sales you would need to generate in order to pay for a new one would be $6,250. By the way, those sales are on top of your existing sales. You need those sales just to get you back to break-even where you were before you bought the new compressor.

Thinking about the value of a dollar in these terms can have a drastic effect on the bottom line. If you get into the habit of thinking in terms of related sales to pay for an item, it is a whole different story when you make a purchase.

Save By Setting Up Exclusive Deals

In addition to thinking in this new way, you have on your side the economy of scale. In other words, multiply savings by how often you purchase a particular item in a year. We used to buy different specialty coffees at our brewpub in Salida, Colorado from a number of purveyors with an average price of $6.10 per pound. Then, we set up a deal with one specific roaster promoting their coffees exclusively and in return received our own special blend for $5.45 per pound. That is a savings of .65 per pound. We typically went through 300 pounds a year so that is a savings of $195, or the same as an additional $2,437.50 in sales!

I'm sure you can think of plenty of things that you will use a lot, from trash bags to coasters. If you can save just five cents on an item that you purchase thousands of per year that can translate into the equivalent of thousands of dollars in additional sales that you didn't need.

Forced Savings Account

Now for something radical: set up a forced savings account. It doesn't matter how small, just know that on a certain day of the month a specific amount of money is going out of your checking account and into an interest bearing one. It follows the old rule to "pay yourself first".

Businesses and individuals don't usually do this, however. There is a very simple reason for doing this. If you do not do this, the year will slip by and at the end of the year, what will you have to show for your efforts? If you had to write a check every month, you might also find an excuse not to write that check. Either you would feel that there was not enough money in the checking account, or you might have a large purchase coming up that you wanted to save the money for. If the money comes out of your account in the form of an automatic transfer however, you will never even think about it.

Start with something small just to see how it goes, even $100 a month. This is easy to do for almost any business. What does it mean? It means that at the end of the year you will have $1,200 plus interest to do whatever you like with. Use it to pay for a vacation, employee bonus, or a new piece of equipment (that you didn't have to borrow to buy, thus saving even more interest). The fact is that you have the cash and therefore have the freedom to choose what to spend it on. Without the forced monthly savings, you would have spent that money during the course of the year and have no idea what you spent it on.

Any bank can set this up for you. You will find that the interest is better if it is invested in treasury securities, or money market accounts. Talk to a stockbroker or investment advisor about different options. You want the money to be invested in something that is safe, and that you can write checks from, in case there is an emergency and you need to get at those funds. Now the fun part is watching this account grow every month. It doesn't take long before you start to figure ways to increase the amount of money that is taken out every month. In fact, every penny you save now has a useful place to go. Hopefully, it won't be too hard to justify $2,000 a month into this account, or more. Now we are talking real money.

There is nothing wrong with creating wealth. It is only through profit that you provide capitol to grow and pay wages. We are not talking greed here. It is only being responsible for your own financial wellbeing. As you save and invest, you start to live on the other side of the interest hill and your money starts earning, without you working for it. It is a beautiful thing to watch. Eventually your money is earning more than you need to cover your monthly living expenses. So guess what? You don't have to work anymore, at least not for a paycheck, but maybe for more altruistic reasons like volunteering for organizations you believe in. There has to be more to following a business system other than just good business. If should be financially rewarding as well.

Conclusion

Some will say that breweries are a fad, or that we already have too many. We finally have over 2,000 breweries in the U.S., the same number we had in 1900, but it doesn't even come close to the 7,000 wineries in the U.S. There is lots of room for growth.

I am sure there will be shakeouts from time to time. These will be mainly people who got into the brewery business to make a quick buck on the hot new thing, or the folks who just spent too much in the first place.

For the person with a passion for creating great beer who opens a brewery with low overhead, and a tight business system, they can expect a long future in this business. From one brewer to another "welcome to the fraternity!"

Cheers.
Tom

INDEX

A. Local Licensing Authorities

U.S.

Alabama

www.abcboard.state.al.us

Alaska

www.dps.state.ak.us/abc

Arizona

www.azll.com

Arkansas

www.arkansas.gov/dfa/abcadministration/index.html

California

www.abc.ca.gov

Colorado

www.revenue.state.co.us/liquor_dir/liquor.html

Connecticut

www.dcp.state.ct.us/licensing/liquor.html

Delaware

www.dabcte.state.de.us/dabcpublic/indez.jsp

District of Columbia

www.abra.dc.gov/abra/site/default.asp

Florida

www.state.fl.us/dbpr/abt/forms/index.shtml

Georgia

www.state.ga.us/departments/dor/alcohol/index.shtml

Hawaii

www.co.honolulu.hi.us/liq

Idaho

www.state.id.us/isld

Illinois

www.state.il.uslcc

Indiana

www.in.gov/atc

Iowa

www.iowaabd.com

Kansas

www.ksrevenue.org/abc.htm

Kentucky

www.abc.ppr.ky.gov

Louisiana

www.ncsla.org/louisiana.htm

Maine

www.maineliquor.com

Maryland

www.comp.state.md.us/main/contactus.asp

Massachusetts

www.mass.gov/abcc

Michigan

www.michigan.gov/cis

Minnesota

www.dps.state.mn.us/alcgamb/alcgamb.html

Missouri

www.mdlc.state.mo.us

Montana

www.discoveringmontana.com/revenue

Nebraska

www.nol.org/home/NLCC

Nevada (alcohol permits are regulated by each individual county)

www.tax.state.nv.us

New Hampshire

www.webster.state.nh.us/liquor/index.shtml

New Jersey

www.state.nj.us/lps/abc/index.html

New Mexico

www.rld.state.nm.us/agd/index.htm

New York

www.abc.state.ny.us

North Carolina

www.ncabc.com

North Dakota

www.state.nd.us/taxdpt/alcohol

Ohio

www.liquorcontrol.ohio.gov/liquor.htm

Oklahoma

www.able.state.ok.us

Oregon

www.olcc.state.or.us

Pennsylvania

www.lcb.state.pa.us

Rhode Island

www.dbr.state.ri.us/liquor_comp.html

South Carolina

www.sctax.org/default.htm

South Dakota

www.state.sd.us/drr2/revenue.html

Tennessee

www.state.tn.us/abc

Texas

www.tabc.state.tx.us/contact/maps.htm

Utah

www.alcbev.state.ut.us

Vermont

www.state.vt.us/dle

Virginia

www.abc.state.va.us

Washington

www.liq.wa.gov/default.asp

West Virginia

www.wvbca.com

Wisconsin

www.dor.state.wi.us

Wyoming

www.revenue.state..wy.us

Canada

Alberta

www.aglc.gov.ab.ca

British Columbia

www.bcliquorstores.com

Manitoba

www.mlcc.mb.ca

Newfoundland

www.nfliquor.com

New Brunswick

www.nbliquor.com

Nova Scotia

www.nsliquor.ns.ca

Ontario

www.lcbo.com

Prince Edward Island

www.gov.pe.ca/tourism/plcc-info/index.php3

Quebec

www.saq.com

Saskatchewan

www.slga.gov.sk.ca

Northwest Territories

www.gov.nt.ca

Yukon Territory

www.ylc.ca

B. Brewing Resources

www.forgework.com Direct Fired Kettles, Mash Tuns & Mills

www.probrewer.com/classifieds Place to find everything from hops, equipment, to brewers and investors.

ZhengAnnabel wzshuangding@hotmail.com Good Chinese Equipment

www.ager-tank-equipment.com A huge inventory of equipment, but no prices listed.

www.dairyeng.com Great place to fine used tanks. They can also make any special parts you need and get it to you within two days.

www.craigslist.org Sometimes you can find pumps and dairy tanks.

www.ebay.com Same as craigslist, but easier to search.

www.gwkent.com Great place to buy new brewing parts and equipment.

www.stpats.com Same as GW Kent. You can compare prices between the two.

www.foxxequipment.com For small beer parts and draft systems

www.taphandles.com Tap handles of all kinds.

www.chrislanceramics.com Ceramic tap handles

www.brew-magic.com Kegs and keg parts.

www.micromatic.com Draft towers and draft supplies

www.brewerssupplygroup.com Malt and Hops

www.fivestarchemicals.com Cleaning and process chemicals

www.storeitcold.com A device to inexpensively create your own cooler

www.sundaylounge.com First class logo design

www.hopunion.com The go-to people for hops

www.hambydairysupply.com Good source for heat exchangers

www.egrandstand.com Growlers Glasses, Logo Tee Shirts

www.glaciertanks.com Serving Tanks

www.ukbrewing.com Real Ale Equipment

www.birkocorp.com Brewing Chemicals

www.countrymaltgroup.com Malt and Hops

www.usfoodsculinaryequipmentandsupplies.com Restaurant

C. Brewery Examples

602 Clinton St.

Ridgway, Colorado 81432

Owners: Tom & Sandy Hennessy
Opened: 2008
Construction Cost: $185,000
Brewing Equipment: $35,000

How did you come up with the idea to start your own brewery?

This was our 6th brewery. We built and owned the first four while owning the Il Vicino Wood Oven Pizza Chain. We sold that in 1999 and took a sabbatical. Then we opened Palisade Brewery in Palisade Colorado in 2003. This was a 20 BBL production brewery. Someone offered to buy it so we sold it in 2005. Production brewing isn't as much fun in my book as pub brewing.

Then while hiking through the Highlands of Scotland I was inspired by the cozy small pubs and breweries scattered about the hills. I thought something small and quaint would work in Ridgway, the town we had moved to in 2006. We found a small (1,200 sq. ft.) space and started to work.

What was the first thing you did?

After purchasing the building I brought the local building inspector into the space and showed him some drawings of what I planned to do. I asked if there were any issues that he could see, and when I felt there were none, I gave my drawings to a local architect to have them drawn up.

What were you doing before you started your brewery?

Sandy and I had taken time off and worked as seasonal park rangers. But the point of this question is that I had been in the restaurant business for 30 years, which included brewing beer. Dong another brewery just involved following the steps outlined in this book.

What did you spend on plumbing, electrical, general construction and total cost to open the doors?

About $150,000. This was because the space was not a restaurant previously. It was just a large open space. We put in all new plumbing and electric. The building is old, built in 1915, and the floor joists in one part of the space sat right on the ground. This is where I located the brewery, because I could take the floor out, lay in the floor drains and put down a cement floor sloped properly so that everything flows to the drain.

We also added 30 hot water solar tubes to the roof with about 200 gallons of storage that fed the on demand hot water heater. This system costs $15,000 but we felt it was worth it and our energy bills bear that out.

In addition we built a new handicap restroom. All of the interior walls had to be added. There was a small basement but the only way to get to it was from a hatch in the floor and then you would jump down into it. So we added stairs so that we could use it freely for storage and office space.

A Warm Pub On A Cold Night

What as the cost of your brewing equipment and what size was it?

I found a 7BBL kettle, pump, heat exchanger, mill and two Grundy tanks on ProBrewer classifieds for $7,000. Turns out it was Dean Rouleau, my old friend who helped me make the Frankenbrew video in 1995. It was a sweet deal.

For fermenters I found two old Specific Mechanical tanks at Dairy Engineering in Denver for $3,000 each (since then I have replaced these). Also sitting in their yard was a small, 150 gallon, dairy tank that cost $500. I had them raise the sides to make it hold 200 gallons. The total cost was $750 for that. I made the false bottom using copper tubes left over from the building process. I bought another Grundy tank for

\$1,500 (eventually I found a 4th one), and a used glycol chiller. The balance of what I spent was on pieces and parts that I bought new from either GW Kent, or St. Pats of Texas, depending on who had the best price at the time.

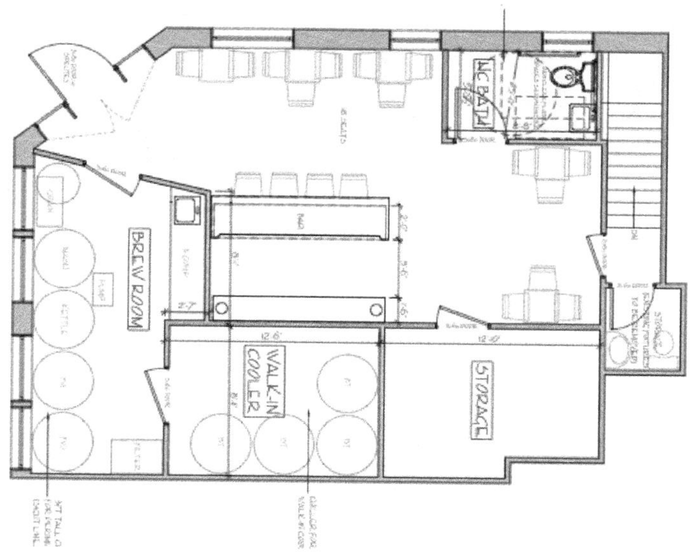

Original Colorado Boy Layout

Pub Area

Where did the money come from?

All the money came from our savings. I am bad about trusting the stock market and have always believed in controlling the stock I invest in. By investing in our own company we have complete control. I realize this option isn't available to everyone, but it came from years of saving. We essentially lent the money to the company and charge it interest. It makes for a great investment. Why let the banks make the money?

Describe what it looked like.

When we first acquired the space it was just one big open room. It had three great advantages however; first it was a corner lot so visibility was good. Second it had these huge windows that let in lots of light onto beautiful wood floors and high ceilings. Third, it already had an old bar built in the late 1800's that became the centerpiece in the pub.

How did you choose your location?

Even though Ridgway is an old western town (the original True Grit was filmed here) there are not a lot of old buildings. Sandy and I wanted something that would lend itself to a warm pub atmosphere. Our preference was an old building with high ceilings, brick and wood floors. This space had been sitting empty for some time and the price was cheap for Ridgway at the time. Ideally it would have been great if the space had previously been a restaurant but there weren't any available. In this case the look of the space trumped its prior use.

Describe an interesting story about your opening.

Have you grown since opening?

We have expanded from within. When we started we had a manufacturing license. This allowed us to make our own beer, have a tasting room, and distribute it. So the only thing we sold were beer and merchandise, and we gave away popcorn. That was way too limiting in a town with a population of only 800, so after a year we changed our license out to a brewpub license. In Colorado this license allows you to sell wine and hard spirits (we chose not to) as long as 15% of your sales is food. We changed our storage area behind the bar to a small kitchen and made Panini sandwiches. This helped a bit but it still wasn't serious food.

Starting in 2010 we remodeled the kitchen so that we could fit a good pizza oven in and started doing artisan pizzas with everything made from scratch and using high-end ingredients. That has caused our sales to increase by 40%.

In the brewery we added cask ales to our list of beers and made it a signature feature in the pub. The two fermenters we started with were replaced with Letina tanks that work better in a small space. This has allowed enough extra space to install a hot liquor tank, and we are in the process of installing a mill with an auger and grist hydrator, which will make brew day a little easier and save us money over buying pre-milled grain.

What would you do differently if you did it all over again?

I would have started with food right away. It has made all the difference in our little pub. I would have also built the walk in cooler rather than buy one. That way I could have utilized the high ceilings and double stacked tanks in the same floor space, which would have doubled our storage capacity, allowing a larger amount of ales and lagers to be on tap at any one time. Like every brewer I have talked to, the number one complaint is not having enough space.

1810 SE 10th Ave

Portland, OR 97214

Owner: Mike Wright
Opened: 2010
Construction Cost: $15,000
Brewing Equipment: $75,000

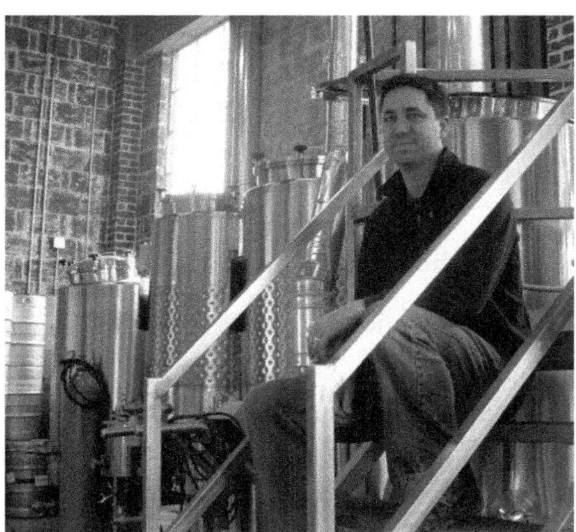

Mike Wright

How did you come up with the idea to start your own brewery?

In many ways it found me. I started home brewing and was almost instantly hooked. The hobby continued to grow over the years. Then in 2009 I decided to see if I could get commercially licensed in my garage. To my surprise, that is exactly what happened. By the summer of 2010, I was legally able to produce beer in my garage and sell it to bars, and restaurants in Oregon. I collected some new and some used equipment and was soon running a nano brewery out of my residential garage-1 barrel (BBL) at a time.

I started to get a few regular accounts and it quickly became clear that a nano brewery was not going to work with my lifestyle and new found ambitions. So, I started to plan out a modest expansion to a new commercial space and a 7 BBL system. That plan was realized on September 15, 2011, when we brewed the first batch of beer on the new system as The Commons Brewery.

What was the first thing you did?

The first thing I did was order a kettle. That act committed me to this venture in my mind.

What were you doing before you started your brewery?

What I did before, I continue to do. I have a day job as an IT project manager. The vast majority of my career has revolved around enterprise custom software projects. It is varied and interesting work, and has taught me a lot about business. That business experience has served me well.

What did you spend on plumbing, electrical, general construction and total cost to open the doors?

Water, natural gas plumbing and construction build-out was about $15,000. I purposely chose a location that required a limited amount of build-out. This was not a guarantee by any means, but I was lucky enough to find a place that needed very little work to bring the brewery and tasting room online. Having said that, I also kept the build-out to the minimum necessary.

What as the cost of your brewing equipment and what size was it?

I purchased a 7 BBL system. The system was built by Practical Fusion; a very small fabrication shop in the Portland metro area. Since this is not a turnkey system, I don't have one nice, clean invoice. I procured all the various parts from chiller, to control panel from different vendors. I can safely say the system is in the neighborhood of $70-80K. And by "system" I am including everything that allows me to turn raw materials into drinkable beer. Not buying the turnkey system allowed me to save a lot of money. And, it also provided a significant challenge for someone who had not previously run a commercial brewery.

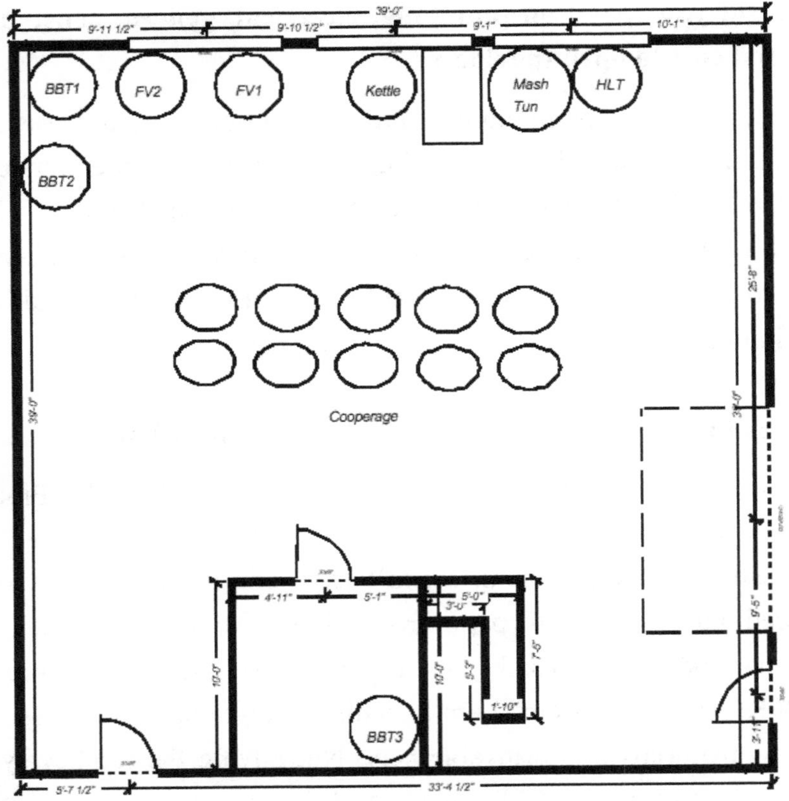

Commons Brewery Layout

Where did the money come from?

I was able to rob (read borrow) money from my retirement savings. The 12 plus years of IT work leading up to this moment ended up building a foundation that I was able to tap into. The upside of this is I don't have to answer to any investors, or carry large amounts of debt. The downside is I could be digging my own grave if it does not work out in the end.

Describe what it looked like.

My space was very nice to start. The building owner took 8000 sq. ft. of his Roof Supply building and revamped it into 5 relatively small commercial units. He stubbed out all new utilities. The concrete floors were ground down and had been polished. There is a commons area for all tenants, which includes two ADA bathrooms. I have a 10' x 10' roll-up door that allows for easy access. All told, the space was in remarkably good condition coming in. Light-years ahead of many other spaces I had been looking at.

How did you choose your location?

I wanted to be in "close-in Southeast Portland". I've lived in SE Portland for the better part of 15 years and really align with the culture. "Close-in SE" is a very desirable area, which made it challenging to find a location. It turns out that I hit a bull's eye on the desired location. I'm exactly where I wanted to be.

Describe an interesting story about your opening.

We were so focused on getting the brewery up and running and making our first few batches of beer that the tasting room sat idle with a handful of jobs not yet complete. I had a number of people asking me when the grand opening was going to be; this happened with pretty regular rhythm for a few months. The "grand" part of their question was a pressure I wasn't ready to live up to. At some point with beer in the tanks, and the end of the year approaching, I got The Commons crew together (all three of us) and hammered out a punch list of things to get done so we could open the tasting room. We accomplished all the items on this list in about a week and decided to open the doors that weekend (December 3rd, 2011).

No fanfare and lacking all things grandiose, we just opened the doors and decided to see what would come next. Leading into that weekend we already had plans to brew on Saturday, December 3rd and so we did. The doors were open at 4pm, and we were just putting the finishing touches on our clean up when people started to stack up outside the front door. We scrambled to finish up and poured our first beer a little after 4:00 pm that day. It turned out to be a really busy night. I quickly figured out how to work the bar, and wash glasses (by hand), while stopping to chat with patrons. All told it was a great success.

Have you grown since opening?

At the time I'm writing this we've been open two months. So, no we haven't grown yet, but do have another brite tank on order, have just submitted another order for kegs, and are already wishing we had more space. Actually, I've just rented some additional cold storage for our bottled beers.

What would you do differently if you did it all over again?

Well, with everything I've learned I would have purchased a 10-15BBL system, and at least double the space and double the cold storage. Saying that, I know that first I had to go through the process and gain the confidence and knowledge I have now.

Commons Brewery

104 W Orgain Ave, Wibaux, MT

Owners: Jim Divine, Sandon Stinnett & Russ Houck
Opened: 2009
Construction Cost: $125,000
Brewing Equipment: $20,000

Jim Devine, Sandon Stinnett, Russ Houck

How did you come up with the idea to start your own brewery?

My business partner Sandon Stinnett and myself were in a homebrew club in Glendive for about 10 years. The club dwindled down to three members for the last 4 or 5 years. We started inviting friends and other folks from the community, to our homebrew parties to sample our brews. For about 2 years people started asking us to provide beer for certain events, etc. Then after a night of pints, Sandon and I decided to pursue opening a brewery.

What was the first thing you did?

The first thing we did was look for a location. I had commuted from Wibaux to Glendive (30 miles) for almost 13 years so we agreed to look for a place in Wibaux. We asked the clerk and recorder's office if there was a building sitting vacant that had a walk-in cooler. They directed us to Russ Houck, our eventual third partner, who owns our current location. To become an owner, Russ offered to renovate the building to code and add some seed money for 20% ownership.

What were you doing before you started your brewery?

Before we opened the brewery I was a social worker working with kids, adults, and families dealing with developmental disabilities. Sandon was also a social worker dealing in child protection. We both had more than 12 years on the job.

What did you spend on plumbing, electrical, general construction and total cost to open the doors?

The renovation of this 1914 building took 18 months to complete. The building was literally falling off the foundation. Sandon, my wife, Sandra Devine, and myself logged more than 4000 hours of labor. We did everything we could that didn't need to be done by a commercial contractor. One of our toughest tasks was finding a commercial plumber to accept the job. We live in a rural area and they are difficult to come by. That was the biggest delay. When the project was completed, Russ had spent $125, 000 in renovation costs along with our labor.

What was the cost of your brewing equipment and what size was it?

We were aware that a small brewery, Milestown Brewing Company, was closing in Miles City, Mt. It was a 4.5 bbl extract system that came with 75 kegs. We purchased it for $12,000! We have since added 2 9bbl, 1 10 bbl, and 1 15bbl fermenters, as well as a 10bbl brite tank and many more kegs. We ordered a new 10bbl brew-house, which has been in operation about 3 months. We are happy, but still trying to keep up! The brew-house alone was $60K!

Where did the money come from?

Russ privately paid for the renovation. The money to get us operating was another story. Sandon and I went from bank to bank to bank, only to be lectured on what a bad idea this was. Jeff Walters, was my private financial consultant and longtime friend. He was also working with Don Tvetene, a businessman that Jeff grew up with in Terry. MT. Jeff knew of our difficulties finding financing to open the brewery, and suggested that we talk to Don. Don had some money to invest and liked the idea of a small business opening in Wibaux, a town losing population every year. So we pitched the idea and Don invested $50,000.

Describe what it looked like?

The building last housed a grocery store in 1986. Russ was just using it for storage. The only thing working was the walk-in cooler. The south facing wall was literally off the foundation. We also had to add an addition for the utility room and bathrooms.

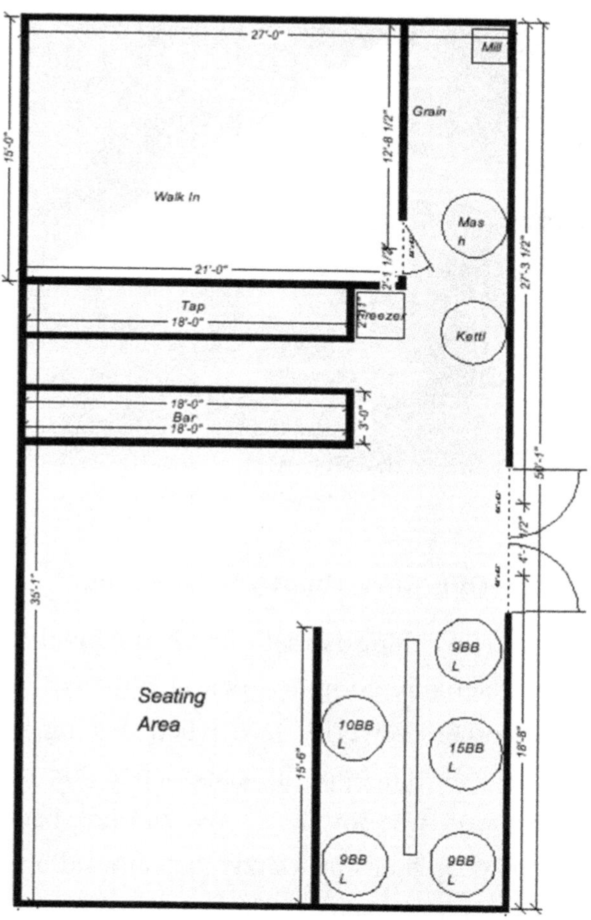

How did you choose your location?

We are in a rural area but we are right on I-94. We are the first town in Montana when a person is heading west out of North Dakota. This has proven to be a huge advantage to us, getting tourists off the interstate.

Beaver Creek Brewery

Describe an interesting story about your opening.

The most interesting thing is that our town council was so excited that a business was actually going to open in Wibaux. We always hear of the nightmares other breweries face when dealing with their local municipalities. It was the opposite experience for us. The actual opening of the brewery was low key. We had one beer on tap and it was mostly curious people or our friends that showed up. Someone did do a blog about our first day and our first batch of beer!

Have you grown since opening?

All we have been doing is growing at a rapid pace! We have gone from producing 220 barrels (bbls) in 2009, our first full year, to 406 in 2010, to 651 in 2011. We started out self-distributing to 12 accounts and have gone to having 3 distributors in two states, Montana and North Dakota. We are now available from Bismarck, ND to Billings, MT.

Our website www.beavercreekbrewery.com has a current list of locations where our beer can be found. We only package kegs.

Seating Area Beaver Creek Brewery

What would you do differently if you did it all over again?

We would have definitely started with a bigger system. There was a brewery that had closed in Dickinson, ND, which is just 75 miles away. They had real nice equipment and a 10 bbl system. They wanted $85,000 for the whole thing. At the time we thought that was a lot of money and we were opening the whole place for $50,000 so we passed. I kick myself every week for that decision!

615 South 1st Avenue, Pocatello, ID

Owners:Penny Pink

Opened: 1996

Construction Cost:$0

Brewing Equipment: $5,000

Penny Pink

How did you come up with the idea to start your own brewery?

I'll blame that on my husband. Sometime in late 1995, my husband made what were likely two totally unrelated comments. His first remark was that I needed to get another job to help supplement our income. Second, was that I needed to get all my home brewing stuff out of the house. My hobby had gotten completely out of control. There were stacks of grain in the dining room, bottles everywhere, carboys with fermenting beer on the kitchen counters. Fermentations would kick off in the middle of the night in the kitchen and the rumbling, blurb, blurb, blurb of the CO2 blowing off could be heard from our adjacent bedroom often waking us out of a dead sleep. Perhaps what precipitated the remark was when he walked in and I was trying to bottle some beer with my new counter-pressure bottle filler and the beer had just exploded all over the kitchen and it was dripping off the ceiling, off the end of my nose and running down the front of all the kitchen cabinets. He was not amused.

What was the first thing you did?

Somehow I linked these two remarks and got to thinking… hum, wonder if I could start a microbrewery in Pocatello? That would get my brewing stuff out of the house and perhaps generate some income. First I did some research to find out if there were any microbreweries in Pocatello. Turns out there had been a REALLY small, essentially home-brew scale microbrewery in a small sub-leased space inside a local sports bar. The owner of the sports bar was interested in talking to me about opening another brewery in the same space. So, I dug into the regulations to figure out how to get licensed and bonded to brew commercially and got that process started. Then I went to work shopping for scrap metal tanks I could convert into a small brewery.

What were you doing before you started your brewery?

My undergraduate degrees are in biology and chemistry and my masters' degree is in Hazardous Waste Management, an interdisciplinary MS degree in biology and engineering. Most of my career up to that point had been spent doing analytical chemistry, microbiology and environmental regulatory compliance.

What did you spend on plumbing, electrical, general construction and total cost to open the doors?

Virtually nothing. The only thing I remember that we had to do to renovate the space I subleased in the sports bar (Dudley's Sports Bar and Grill) was to stub in a couple of water lines for a three tub sink and run a gas line into the room to fire the brew kettles. Somehow I think we got most of that work done on trade from a friend of the owner of the sports bar.

What was the cost of your brewing equipment and what size was it?

Bottom line: first year capital expenses, including a semi-load of kegs, were under $5K. As stated previously, the original system was designed to brew 2 bbl per batch. I eventually reconfigured the system to crank out 3 bbls per batch and brewed well over 1000 batches of beer on that system.

Where did the money come from?

From what I remember I had managed to scrape together some meager funds off one of my credit cards and got a small loan from one of my friends. All total for equipment, licenses and other start-up costs

I only spent around $5K initially to get the operation off the ground the first year.

Describe what it looked like?

My first brewing system was cobbled together out of a bunch of scrap metal tanks I got from Metro Metals in Portland, Oregon. I spent a couple of months drinking beer, scratching my head figuring out how to fill in orifices and make new ones to re-configure the tanks into a brewing system and teaching myself how to do stainless steel finish work. Eventually with some help from friends that could weld, including my husband, I had polished up the tanks and turned them into a 2 bbl brew house and two 2 bbl dish bottomed fermenters. Then it was a simple matter to move the system down to the sports bar and put her to work.

How did you choose your location?

I think it would be more accurate to say that the location chose me. Because someone else had already had a small micro-brewery in the space and all the various government agencies had licensed it, opening another brewery in the same spot presented less hurdles than I thought I would face in another location. It also gave me a guaranteed first customer. I had 7 taps in the sports bar, plus a tap for the Sarsaparilla we make. I think I had about 500 square feet of space for the brewery sub-leased in what used to be the old historic Federal building that housed the old post office. My malt room had been the old postal vault with steel doors like you would see at a bank and 15-inch thick concrete walls. My original brewing system didn't have any pumps or motors, so it was a pretty simple operation that didn't require much infrastructure. I didn't even have floor drains. If something spilled I had what I would call a "cleaning opportunity." I ground all my malt by hand with a hand crank on my mill, transferred liquid between tanks in 5 gallon buckets and carbonated the beer by shaking CO2 into my old Golden Gate kegs by laying them on the floor in the walk-in cooler in the basement and shaking them 50 times over a couple of days at 18 psi.

Describe an interesting story about your opening

The initial opening of the brewery in July of 1996 has got to be the softest "soft opening" of a business in history. I had brewed several batches of beer and had the sports bar stocked up with inventory prior to our official "opening." There was a hand-written white board sign in the window of the room that housed the brewery in the back of the sports bar that proclaimed its new identity as "Portneuf Valley Brewing." Even the article in the paper about the new brewery opening in town made comment of the simplistic sign in the window of the old video arcade room. As soon as we got the business open I took off for a long planned three-week vacation to Alaska with the family. That is the longest vacation I've had since opening. Since then most of my vacations you could count in hours not days.

Have you grown since opening?

Oh my, hell, yes! In the spring of 2002, Dudley's Sports Bar and Grill went out of business in the wake of 9/11. The owner of the building gave me three months to get out. This precipitated some major changes. My husband gave me an ultimatum. Either shut the business down or go back to work doing what I was trained to do to support the family and the business. I chose the latter. I had bought the bottling plant of what used to be East Idaho Brewing Company over on the other side of the railroad tracks in the Historic Warehouse District in 1999. I had spent 3 years with my sons gutting out the shell of the 9000 square foot warehouse. It was going to cost me more money than I had to get enough of the building renovated to move the brewery in, so I had to go back to work to support the business. I socked everything I made working another job for the next 4 years into subsidizing the business and boot-strapping my way through stage after stage of renovations to finally get the pub open so we could serve beer by the glass. That was 2005 and the business started to hold its own to the point that I could demonstrate to the bank that I was worthy of a loan. We needed funds to complete the renovations to open a kitchen in order to operate as a full- fledged restaurant and brewery. My husband told me I could quit my other job and go back to running and working the business full time if I paid off all our personal debt. By 2006 I had the business on solid financial footing and had all our personal debt paid off. I took everything extra I made for the next three years and pumped it into upgrading the brewing system. Over three years I replaced the old system with REAL sanitary brewing equipment including; a really efficient 3 bbl brew house, four 4 bbl fermenters, a 4 bbl bright tank, three 6-7 bbl fermenters, three 6 bbl bright tanks and nine 6 bbl serving tanks. The business now operates as a thriving brewpub with revenue a couple orders of magnitude over what I generated 16 years ago. We have live entertainment in the loft on the second floor four nights per week. We are open for lunch and dinner Monday thru Saturday. We have ten beers we make on tap as well as our house-made Carrie Nation Sarsaparilla. As one customer commented to me recently, "PVB has become a community center for Pocatello." Given that one of my main objectives in opening a brewery in Poky was to "liven the place up" that comment made my day.

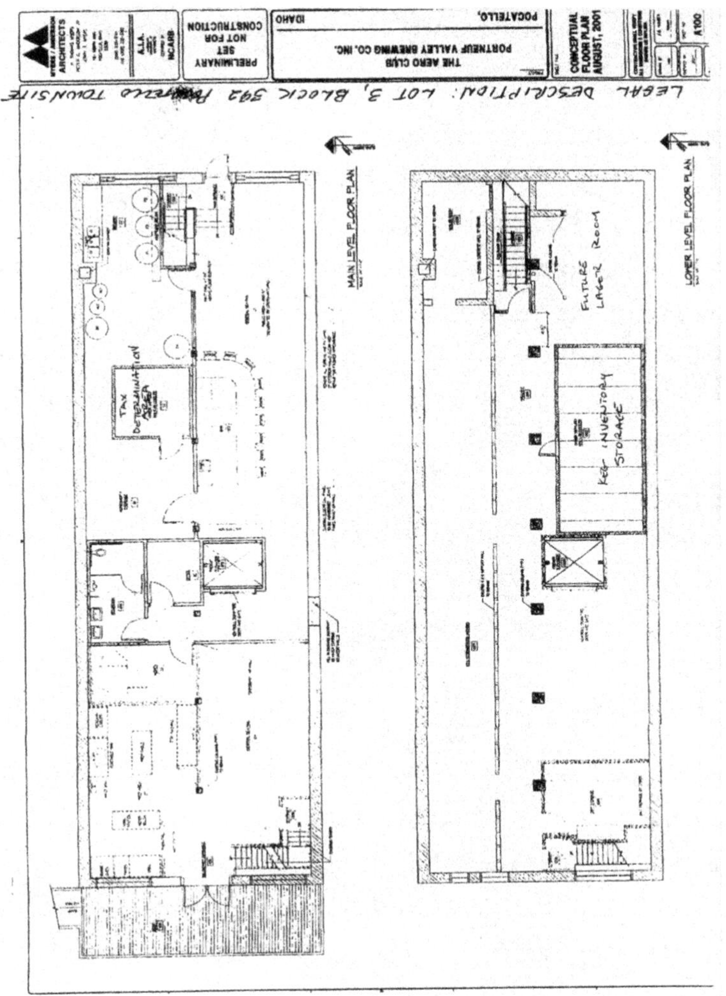

PVB Current Brewery Layout

What would you do differently if you did it all over again?

Write a business plan FIRST! My game plan initially was to start small and learn the business, learn the market, and refine my product line before I invested a ton of money. In retrospect I still think that was a good strategy. I have a REALLY tough demographic in that my market is saturated with non-alcohol drinkers, so starting small and slowly building the business as I could afford to do it was a good strategy for me at the time. Of course it all would have been MUCH easier if I had a lot of cash to start with, but it's been a grand adventure and one of the biggest challenges of my long and diverse career. I did ultimately write a business plan and that was crucial for guiding the phases of building out where the business is today. Now it's time to re-write the plan and chart the growth for the next 15 years as I cruise towards retirement age. What will the next chapter be???

Personal footnote:

I could not have done what I've done building the business to where it is now 16 years later without the help of literally hundreds of friends and supporter to which I am deeply in debt. They are WAY too numerous to list. I have learned that owning a brewery is not so much a job as a lifestyle. The beer is just the glue that holds it all together.

Owners: Jay & Lori Wince
Opened: 2007
Construction Cost: $96,000
Brewing Equipment: $12,100

Jay & Lori Wince

How did you come up with the idea to start your own brewery?

We fell in love with Craft Beer back in the early 90's after we started to travel more extensively in the U.S. That led us to home brewing. After becoming pretty seriously involved in the homebrew community and starting to compete with our beer in the early 2000's we started to research the idea of doing it commercially.

What was the first thing you did?

The first thing we did was to begin the search for equipment. At that time equipment was more readily available and the prices were good. After the surge in the late 90's and then the rash of closings, systems were still out there at affordable prices. We actually bought our system before we had a location secured.

What were you doing before you started your brewery?

Lori was and still is a newspaper journalist. Jay worked in a commercial bakery as a production supervisor and continued to work there until the end of 2011. During this time we ran the brewery and maintained our jobs as well.

What did you spend on plumbing, electrical, general construction and total cost to open the doors?

Our total cost to commence brewing in July of 2007 including all build-out and overhead costs (rent, utilities, equipment, contractors, etc.) was just under $75,000. We continued to finish out the taproom. By the time the taproom opened in January of 2008 our total cost was just over $108,000.

Electrical costs including taproom opening, were about $12,500 with us doing a lot of work under our electrician's guidance (i.e.

installing fixtures, pulling wire, etc.) Plumbing costs were just about $6500.

The remaining costs were for other small contractors (tile, concrete, etc.) and equipment, furnishings and other things required for building the brewery and pub. As stated, much of the work was done by us and by our friends. Some improvements were made at the expense of the building owner.

What was the cost of your brewing equipment and what size was it?

Our brewing system is a CDC system built by John Cross in 1997. The brew house is a slightly undersized 7 bbl, three vessel system. All fermentation and cellar tanks are 8.5 bbl (10 hl) tanks. Our system was basically complete except for a few missing parts and pieces and a glycol chiller. We bought (stole) the system for $12,100 in 2006.

Where did the money come from?

We did not borrow any money in the conventional sense. We used home equity to fund the project. Since the home was paid for, we were able to get a small business equity loan on our home and cover almost all of our build out expenses and our first few months of overhead. By doing this we knew that even if the venture failed we could still pay our mortgage as usual and not lose our home.

Describe what it looked like?

It was one of the dirtiest spaces we had ever seen. It was a former glass mold machine shop and restoration was going on at the time so we had some hint of what things were going to look like in the rest of the building beyond our leased space.

How did you choose your location?

We wanted an old building, hopefully in the downtown area or nearby. Industrial spaces were high on our list. We looked around but also enlisted the help of our Community Foundation director to suggest space. He happened to own a building that was in the "rehab" stage. He offered to show it to us and offered us a rock bottom square foot price if we signed on early. It was a nice sized open space, had great natural light, was on the river directly across from downtown, had a small patio space and was a blank slate. There was nothing to demolish or tear out. No electric or anything. It was in a zoned planned unit development (PUD), which meant that we did not have to go through any additional zoning for our use as a brewery. There were no churches or schools close to cause any issues. As soon as we walked through the door we knew it was the place.

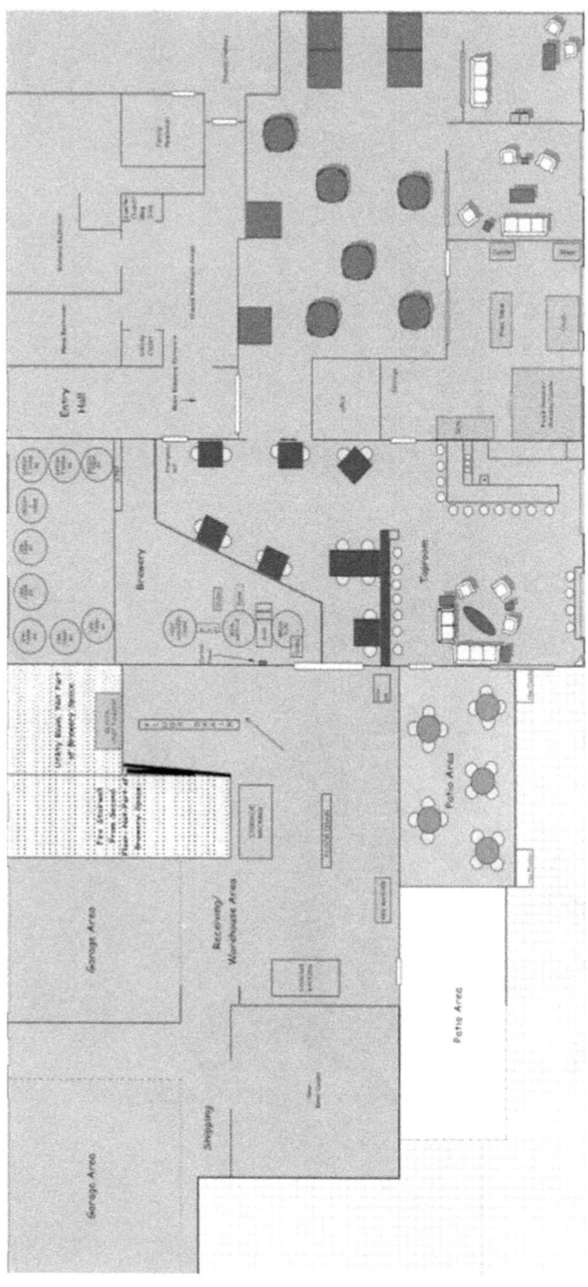
Entry Hall
Brewery
Taproom
Patio Area
Receiving/ Warehouse Area
Garage Area
Shipping
Patio Area
Garage Area

Brewery View Taken From Bar

View From Brewery Into Tasting Area

Describe an interesting story about your opening

After our build out we brewed for about 6 months and distributed kegs locally to help pay our bills while finishing the taproom space. We opened at the end of January and had planned our Grand Opening for the first weekend in March. Food, band and all were retained for the event. It started to snow the day before and by that morning the spring storm had dropped 14-16 inches of snow on the ground. Our town and most of the region was at a standstill and everything was closed or canceled. We had to suck it up and reschedule our Grand Opening about 4 weeks later. We ended up brewing that day instead!! It all worked out. The Grand Opening was packed and it is still one of the busiest days we have ever had.

Have you grown since opening?

Yes we have. Our first half year in operation we brewed 62 bbls. In our first full calendar year of 2008 we did 222 bbls. We increased to 289 bbls in 2009, 408 bbls in 2010 and did 429 bbls in 2011. We increased our seating space by 1700 sq. ft. in 2009 and are currently ready to expand our warehouse/dock space by 1000 sq. ft. this spring. We are also in the build out stage of installing an on premise pizza shop in our current footprint.

We started out with a capacity of about 500 bbls but in 2010 added two new fermenters to expand our capacity to about 850 bbls. These are needed now for our busiest months when we have all 5 "unitanks" filled non-stop.

What would you do differently if you did it all over again?

Not sure what we would change. We did a lot of homework and enlisted the help of many of our professional brewers in the central

Ohio area. We had a good idea going in of what it would take and what to and not to do. This good advice was paramount. Our planning was pretty good but in some cases a bit backwards or unconventional. We basically were opportunistic and waited for things to fall into our laps in some cases. Most of our equipment was used including brewing system, bar coolers, sinks, walk-in coolers, furnishings, etc. We saved literally tens of thousands of dollars by buying good used equipment and by doing most of the build out work ourselves. It's worked out well for us.

Owner: Rich Hennosy
Opened: 2012
Construction Cost: $45,000
Brewing Equipment: $65K-75K

Rich Hennosy

How did you come up with the idea to start your own brewery?

My company had cut our hours back to 32 hours per week. Other firms were laying people off, so I started looking for a business to start, so I could control my own destiny. I came across the probrewer.com website and found people who were starting a brewery. There were very basic questions about their startup, and others with a lot of experience were offering helpful answers. It all seemed very genuine. I was attracted to the fraternity feel of the industry. I then Googled "How to start a brewery," and found the Colorado Boy class. The rest is history.

What was the first thing you did?

The first thing I did was to buy a homebrew kit. I made my first batch, and after opening a few early bottles and being disappointed, I finally opened a properly aged bottle and discovered beer; my very own beer. It was thrilling!

What were you doing before you started your brewery?

I am an IT manager for a retail design firm. Not very challenging; so I was definitely looking for a challenge.

What did you spend on plumbing, electrical, general construction and total cost to open the doors?

I had to do a change of use permit for my location and that meant a lot of unnecessary dollars. I spent $9,000 on plumbing, $8,000 on electric, $15,000 of general construction including the bar and other permanent fixtures, $3,000 on HVAC and $4,000 on an architect. We probably had $3,000 in permits, another $3,000 in furniture. I think the total to open was about $130,000. If you can afford it, I would set aside

$150,000. There are a few items I have to put off until we bring in more money.

What was the cost of your brewing equipment and what size was it?

We have a 6bbl system (probably 1bbl too small) and I probably have $65K-75K in brewing equipment. The biggest surprise was the cost of all the small parts. I probably have $4K in fittings, pipes and gauges, etc.

Where did the money come from?

Most of the money came from life savings and a personal line of credit.

Describe what it looked like.

When we started our space was a hair salon that used to be a gas station back in the 60's. We were lucky when we peeled back the siding. We found old porcelain panels that could be exposed again to easily change the appearance back to a gas station. We put faux garage doors in with lots of windows. Windows are a must. People need to see that they are coming to a brewery and the need to feel welcome.

Tasting Room Buckeye Lake Brewery

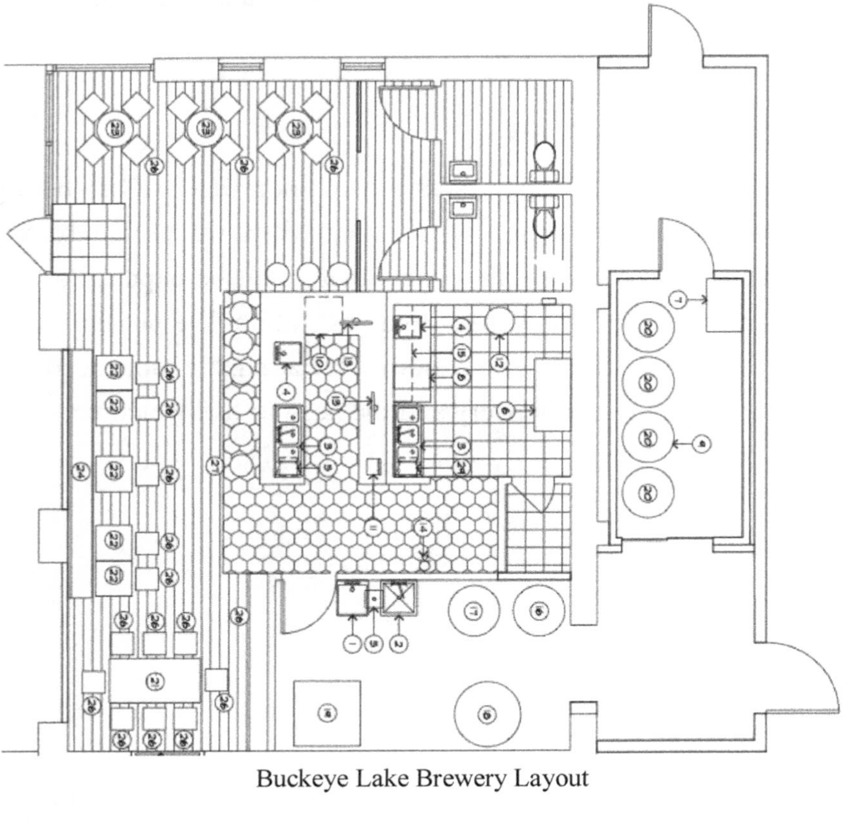

Buckeye Lake Brewery Layout

BREWERY EXAMPLES

Buckeye Lake Brewery Before

Buckeye Lake Brewery After

How did you choose your location?

I immediately thought of the Buckeye Lake Village after taking Tom's class in Ridgway. It is a small tourist town that attracts a lot of people in the summer, a lot like Ridgway. I thought if Tom can make it in a town of 800 and a county of 30,000 with two other breweries 10 minutes away, then I can make it in a town of 2500 with a county population of 250,000 and no other breweries for 30 minutes.

Describe an interesting story about your opening.

The most surprising thing has been the number of people who have come in and thanked me for opening in this small town. Buckeye Lake was once thriving with an amusement park and had seen better days. A brewery, somewhat of an attraction in this town, has been very welcome. I have been greeted with open arms. It is a great feeling.

Have you grown since opening?

We have only been open for six months and have purchased another serving tank and are in the market for another fermenter. My plans to keep revenue up through the winter includes selling to some local bars. This will require the extra fermenter to keep up with demand, which is quite high.

What would you do differently if you did is all over again?

I would probably try to find a location that was previously a restaurant or bar. It would have saved about $15K-20K if I just had to do cosmetic changes not requiring all permits.

Acknowledgements

Many thanks to all my friends in the brewing community who have been teaching me many of the tricks I have accumulated over 20 years of commercial brewing and are in this manual. A Special thanks to Elliott Bell, Rich Hennosy, Jay and Lori Wince, Mike Wright, Penny Pink and Jim Devine for answering questions openly about their breweries. Especially thank you to my wife Sandy who read through the manuscript multiple times and suggested many of the sections in this book. She could have cut and run when I home-brewed my first batch of beer but didn't.

About the Author

Tom Hennessy is the owner of Colorado Boy Pub & Brewery and Colorado Boy Pizzeria & Brewery. They are his sixth and seventh breweries over the past twenty years. He is the creator of Frankenbrew, a cult classic 1995 video on how to build inexpensive breweries. This book is the result of years of teaching many students how to successfully open and operate their own brewery.

CPSIA information can be obtained
at www.ICGtesting.com
Printed in the USA
BVHW071429251119
564771BV00001B/58/P

9 780578 143743